Hot Lemon
and Honey

T0363532

Hot Lemon and Honey

Reflections
for success in
times of change

Catherine DeVrye

Everest Press

First published in 2000 and reprinted 2000 by
Allen & Unwin
Reprinted 2002 by Everest Press. Revised edition 2004
Reprinted 2006, 2007, 2010, 2012, 2014, 2015, 2016
PO Box 559
Manly 1655
NSW, Australia
Phone: (61 2) 9977 3177
E-mail: books@greatmotivation.com
Web: www.greatmotivation.com

National Library of Australia
Cataloguing-in-Publication entry:

DeVrye, Catherine.

Hot lemon and honey: reflections for success in
times of change.

ISBN 0 9580110 2 8.
ISBN-13 978 0 9580110 2 0.

1. Self-actualization (Psychology). 2. Motivation
(Psychology). 3. Conduct of life. 4. Quality of work
life. 5. Figures of speech. I. Title.

158.1

Set in 10/13 pt Rotis Serif
Printed in Australia by SOS Print + Media Group

10 9 8 7 6 5 4

Like the common cold, there is yet no cure for the common ills of the workplace. My hope is that after ingesting Hot Lemon and Honey *you might feel a little better; that your place of work and inner self may seem somewhat more nurtured.*

I don't pretend to prescribe any miracle medication ... just to scribe a few reflections which, with a sip of soothing wisdom, hopefully will help to clear your head of job-related congestion.

Contents

Introduction

'When what used to work at work no longer works, it's time to change our ways of thinking—and think of ways of changing.'

Catherine DeVrye

We're so busy being busy that we hardly have time to think about what we're actually trying to achieve in our work and in our lives.

Have you ever felt swamped with workload? Have you ever wondered how to better balance your professional and personal life? Have you ever wanted a good reason to take some reflective time to think on those days when you don't know whether you're coming or going? Have you ever thought that you're the only person who feels this way? Would you simply like a commonsense perspective? Do you need a little workplace inspiration? If so, this book has been written for you.

It's an easy read that offers encouragement and inspiration to everyone in the workplace today who might be questioning their role. It contains a series of quotable quotes that have been expanded to embrace a wider philosophy in the workplace—a philosophy to nourish the heart, as well as the head.

In his book *Age of Uncertainty*, best-selling British author Charles Handy states (p. 104):

If the research is to be believed, most executives will not have spent more than ten consecutive minutes alone in the working day. They have not had the time to think, even if they know what to think about and where to start.

Most of the chapters in this book can be read in just ten consecutive minutes. They don't for a moment tell you what to think; rather, they are intended as a starting point to prompt you to delve deep into the reservoir of your own thoughts. They are intended to encourage you to at least think—and possibly think a little differently—even if you don't agree with every word. In fact, I worry about people in my presentations who either declare 'It's changed my life' or 'It will never work'. Conversely, I am encouraged by those individuals who have an open mind and healthy scepticism; knowing that no one can change their lives, except themselves. They will truly be victors from change rather than victims of change.

This book can be read in a short time to gain long-term benefits and motivation for both your organisation and yourself. Written specifically for today's busy employee or employer, it's designed to be digested one bite at a time. That way, it's easier to savour the truth in the timeless words of wisdom, presented in a modern-day context.

The 52 chapters have been designed so you can comfortably spend ten minutes reading a chapter each week of the year, then have the remainder of the week to reflect on how these thoughts may apply to you. You can read them in the sequence presented or turn back to the table of contents to choose the quote that may seem most relevant to you at that moment in time.

One of the key issues facing organisations around the world today, both in the private and public sectors, is motivating staff. Many of my clients take motivational quotes from my speeches or customer service books, and put them on employees' pay slips, wall posters, notice boards, t-shirts or screen savers. They seem to like the simplicity of quotes to inspire staff to search for simpler solutions in the workplace.

In talking with thousands of individuals, I've found that, irrespective of whether they are executives or factory floor workers, most people face similar struggles—only in a different context. The worker thinks the bosses never have any problems because they are 'in charge', without understanding that the problems are simply different and somewhat more complex the higher one goes up an organisational ladder. Meanwhile, the boss often wishes to return to the simpler life of not having to manage other people, who seem to be the cause of his or her problems, without remembering the different problems they faced before they were 'in charge'. It's a strange paradox.

Whether speaking in Delhi or Dallas, Singapore or Sydney, Edinburgh or Edmonton, New Zealand or New York, I find there are more similarities than differences when it comes to the human side of workplace issues. Certainly, there are significant cultural differences; however, employees and employers alike, around the world, all share a common desire to provide the best possible livelihood and lifestyle for themselves and their families. In the same way, there are differences within the cultures of individual organisations or even departments within organisations.

Therefore, please recognise that I'm not prescribing answers—just scribing questions that are worth thinking about. *You* have the answer to know what will work best for you! I rather hope that you may disagree with some thoughts because, after all, so much of life is a paradox. Even if you consider that some are old-fashioned quotes that you probably heard from your grandparents, some may seem immutable while, in time, others come to be questioned. For instance, I was brought up to believe:

'Look before you leap' and *'He who hesitates is lost.'*

I must admit that, until writing this book, I hadn't given any consideration to the obvious contradiction when these quotes are placed side by side! However, that doesn't necessarily diminish the wisdom of either, because both—at the appropriate time—may be equally apt.

I also recognise that I could have expanded many of the thoughts in this book and, in some cases, have written an entire book on an individual quote. But that would have defeated the purpose of having a collection of bite-sized chunks of food for thought to snack on, when you don't have time to digest a full-course mental meal.

This book is a collection of timeless quotes and modern-day business philosophy. It's intended to inspire the reader who may normally be too busy to be bothered with ideas—ideas which impact on our professional and personal lives; ideas which touch the heart and the head; ideas which make a difference if we take the time to look at things differently.

Call it meditation if you wish . . . or just-in-time thinking . . . or simply allowing time to clear your mind of clutter to help you better cope with the challenges of your working week.

Anyone who knows me also knows I'm not a morning person so why would I suggest that this book might best be read on a Monday morning, of all times? Or maybe on the weekend before you start your working week. Please feel free to read it anytime but in my observations of the corporate world, government and small business, it seems that the longer the working week goes on, the more turbulent our thoughts become. Wouldn't it be beneficial to at least start out with some refreshing thoughts while your head is still relatively clear from the constant clutter of busy-ness?

That's why Monday morning or a weekend seems a good time for that proverbial wake-up call.

How often do you open your eyes and know that in a few hours, you're likely to have lost that peaceful early dawn feeling? You probably stretch and head for the bathroom where you flush and brush, clearing your body of unwanted waste while getting ready to fill your mind with the mental equivalent.

How about a little brain flossing to remove that build-up of intellectual plaque? Taking a few minutes each morning to shower yourself and your soul not just with hot steamy water but a refreshing stream of consciousness for making work more workable and worthy for the rest of the week; applying some of those good ideas you inevitably get in the shower. We'll avidly listen to the latest tragedies on the morning news or read about them in the paper so why not take less time than reading the paper to reflect on what's important news in your life and what you can do to change your personal headlines?

Before breakfast, many of you will have walked the dog or engaged in your own exercise routine. This book offers some painless pushups for the mind, some sensible stretches to tone those thinking muscles, some encouragement to sit up and take note of what matters. Banish the flab of disempowerment and jog your own thoughts of what works best for you.

As you head to the kitchen or the cafe, it's time for a caffeine-free kick start to the week; like a virtual vitamin supplement for the senses; a low-calorie, fad-free, high-fibre food for thought. Start the day with positive thoughts and don't allow negative self-talk an opportunity to get a grip on you. In fact, why not hum the words of a favourite, upbeat song as you head off to work. Forget Grumpy in *The Seven Dwarfs,* as 'Hi, ho, Hi, ho, it's off to work we go . . .'

Marching to your own tune, may I suggest that, before moving to Chapter 2, you take a moment to think about what you hope to discover by reading this book. You'll be surprised, because that's exactly what you'll find on the following pages.

As you reflect, with an open mind, on the commonsense relevance of these simple thoughts, you'll discover that it is truly possible to make your life worth living as your living is being made if you can remember that:

'When what used to work at work no longer works, it's time to change our ways of thinking—and think of ways of changing.'

1

'Minds are like parachutes—dangerous if not kept open.'

Robert Darrah

These were the words inscribed in my autograph book by our school principal when I was twelve. I probably didn't realise the significance at the time, but years later I appreciate the wisdom of this educator who always encouraged us to ask questions, rather than remain quietly passive to the 'knowledge dumps' of teachers and other adults in authority.

If Mr Darrah were alive today, he would do well as a management consultant because, as grown-ups, we should still ask more childlike questions, rather than simply accepting the status quo. As we age, it's all too easy to fall into the trap of having our thoughts formatted by the way we've always done things.

We get bogged down in old patterns of behaviour because they are comfortable. We usually don't worry about paradigm shifts unless we're actually forced into moderating our manner by some external force such as downsizing or a takeover. It's significant to consider what happens if you remove the letter 'f' from the term 'paradigm shift': we often do find ourselves in the paradigm poo!

When stop signs were first introduced in Melbourne in 1975, an elderly friend firmly believed they only applied to those people who obtained their licences after that date! In spite of warnings, his mind was firmly closed on the subject—and you can well imagine the danger!

Seldom are we faced with such life or death matters in terms of keeping an open mind. Usually, it's the more ordinary events that we may have set ideas about—ideas which prevent us from seeing other opportunities. For example, how would you have liked to be one of the many companies which rejected the Xerox concept, or one of the 600 bankers who turned down Walt Disney, or one of the girls who wouldn't date a geek called Bill Gates because he didn't fit the stereotype?

More commonly in our everyday lives, both professionally and personally, how often do we simply switch off when someone is speaking to us because we have an initial reaction that their ideas aren't consistent with our own? How much more knowledgeable would we be if we could simply listen without bias or preconceived opinions?

I love the old saying:

'If you can't change your mind, are you sure you still have one?'

Often, new people in an organisation will present a refreshing view, only to be completely ignored and told:

'That's not the way we do things around here.'

Yet the more open we are to suggestions, the more likely it is that there will be benefits. Let's look at two examples.

An airline made huge savings as a result of a suggestion from a new employee in the garbage department. He had noticed, when clearing the trays, that most passengers didn't eat their lettuce and suggested the airline get rid of that garnish on the trays. Doing so saved over $1.5 million.

In another instance, a grocery store increased fish sales by listening to a junior employee who had first listened to a customer. A focus group was discussing the fish at the store. One of the women commented that it would be better if it were fresh. The manager defensively assured her that it was indeed fresh. It was trucked from the sea every morning, hygienically wrapped in plastic, put in refrigerated stainless steel containers and any unsold fish was given to a charity at the end of the day. In this case, the customer was wrong but her perception was 100 per cent correct.

A young employee suggested that staff attempt to modify that perception by experimenting: half the fish were wrapped as always, while the other half were simply spread on freshly crushed ice. As you can imagine, the fish on the ice sold better than the packaged product, with additional savings on labour and packaging.

So how can we avoid missing good ideas because our minds aren't as open as they could be? One simple technique is to take a deep breath before immediately responding to a person and offering our own opinion—which we had probably already formulated long before they had even finished their thoughts.

Just as it's dangerous to jump from an airplane and pull the rip cord on the parachute too early, wouldn't it be wise to do as experienced parachutists do and count 1000–1; 1000–2; 1000–3 before jumping in to a conversation with our own thoughts? This would allow some time to actually assimilate what others are saying to us. With a little practice, it's easy to see how effective this can be and recognise that:

'Minds are indeed like parachutes—dangerous if not kept open.'

2

'The only time success comes before work is in the dictionary.'

Vidal Sassoon

Success is something we all strive for, both in our professional and personal lives. Countless books have been written on various ways to succeed, each offering some secret formula or magic recipe for success. Yet there are no instant 'secrets' to success. Certainly, actions such as goal-setting, time management, planning and skilful execution are necessary for each of us to chart our own paths of prosperity. But the overriding factor in achieving that success is to put in the necessary hours and hard work. Lots of people have great ideas but never follow through. As golfer, Gary Player once said:

'The harder I practise, the luckier I get.'

Although wealth may be inherited, individual success cannot be. It is neither genetic nor environmental. Why is it that when two identical twins are raised in the same environment, one can grow to be a successful businessman while the other becomes a homeless alcoholic? The answer lies in the choices each of those individuals made at various stages throughout their lives, even though life initially offered them exactly the same choices.

Success is not something which, once you achieve it, is guaranteed forever. It is something that needs to be constantly worked at—but not 'worked at' to the extent of never being able to enjoy the fruits that come with that success. Success is measured differently by different individuals, but should never be measured purely in a materialistic sense. Truly successful individuals are those who have managed to balance their material well-being with successful relationships with families, friends and colleagues—they look after their physical and spiritual beings. That's not to say that there aren't times when one must work late and miss a gym workout rather than miss an important deadline. After all, it's virtually impossible to be successful in a career today by rigidly working from nine to five and refusing to go that extra distance when required.

Remember, too, that success is not just about *having* things. It's about *doing* things; experiencing different joys for yourself; and experiencing the joy of doing things for others.

Do you ever notice that successful business people are also the ones contributing to community activities—and that they seem to fit more into their day through careful planning of time? Sure they're busy, and like everyone else never seem to have enough hours in the day, but the old maxim is true that if you want a job done, give it to a busy person.

Meanwhile, those less successful are too 'busy' at the pub, the water cooler, in front of the TV, playing computer games or chatting with friends on company time. They might be commenting on someone else's success by saying 'Wasn't he lucky?' or 'Didn't she get all the breaks?' They've never known, or have long forgotten, that . . .

'The only time success comes before work is in the dictionary.'

3

'Customers don't care how much you know until they know how much you care.'

Gerhard Gshwandter

Most organisations espouse customer care without truly appreciating what it really means.

True customer care goes beyond the lip service paid to customer service. It goes beyond product knowledge and politeness. It goes beyond procedures and quality programs. That's not to say that these aren't important ingredients in an overall customer strategy, but the icing on the cake, so to speak, is the genuine care factor. And I don't mean the sickly sweet 'Have a nice day' patter.

Caring encompasses the intellect and the emotion, the head and the heart. It can't be learned in any training manual, yet it is something we've been taught all our lives. Remember when your grandmother or kindly aunt used to say:

'Do unto others as you would have them do unto you.'

This simple Golden Rule can likewise be worth gold to your business. It's a simple customer service maxim and one that a hotel in Perth, Western Australia, certainly practises. I'd arrived at check-in, jet-lagged, with a terrible cold and no voice. As I was supposed to speak to 200 real estate agents the next morning, this was indeed a predicament.

The receptionist pleasantly started her standard greeting, telling me about the pool, golf course, restaurants, etc. Rather impatient to get to bed, I ignored the information and curtly informed her that I simply wanted my key. Reaching my room, I quickly unpacked, had a hot shower and was about to curl up in bed when there was an unexpected knock on the door.

'Room service,' the cheery voice echoed.

Cheerfulness was not what I wanted at that point in time so I tersely informed him that I hadn't ordered room service.

'Yes, we know you haven't, Ms DeVrye. But we also know you're not feeling well so have prepared some hot lemon and honey with our compliments.'

Sure enough, on a silver tray, was exactly what I would have liked if I'd been at home. I sheepishly thanked him as he handed me the tray, which also had some vitamin C and a note from the chef, offering to make anything special I would like for dinner, even if it didn't appear on the menu. What's more, there was another note from the concierge, offering to have medication delivered from a 24-hour chemist.

I felt better already! To think that someone had taken the time to show some genuine care to a stranger in the usually impersonal environment of a hotel, so far from home. The hotel didn't have the best amenities I'd seen in my travels, but, in spending over 70 nights per year in hotels, never have I experienced such heartwarming customer care. And long after I'd forget the marble in the foyer or designer shampoo bottles, I'd always remember the outstanding customer care.

That genuine care wasn't a result of any formal process in their operational procedure manual, but rather a result of the receptionist putting herself in the shoes of a guest and imagining how she would like to be treated if she was in a similar situation.

As soon as she realised I was ill, she no longer tried to impress me with the range of facilities and services. She truly did impress me by coordinating with her colleagues to demonstrate true customer care—by providing hot lemon and honey service straight from the heart!

My voice marginally restored the next day, I addressed the realtors on customer service, using this real-time example of true care. Coincidentally, their training manager had had a similar experience in a New Zealand hotel and as an innovative leader, she suggested that the company adopt 'Hot Lemon and Honey Service' as their theme for the conference and the year, which I'm pleased to report resulted in record sales. Hot lemon and honey . . . the sort of natural nurturing of customers which pays bottom-line dividends once you realise that:

'Customers don't care how much you know until they know how much you care.'

4

'The only person who got everything done by Friday was Robinson Crusoe.'

John Peers

Do you ever feel pressured for time? That you'll never get everything done on your 'to do' list? Or is it more appropriate to ask if you ever feel totally under control and relaxed about the time pressures of today's busy world? If it's the latter, you're certainly unique!

Whatever happened to the so-called increase in leisure time which was muted in the 1970s? It seems that most people of working age are either twice as busy or unemployed. Whatever happened to the happy medium? Most small business owners, especially when starting out, are usually frantically busy or so worried about not being busy, where that next job will come from, that they can't enjoy the quiet time. Fortunately, if they survive, better balance is achieved through time as they learn to plan cash flow for those lulls. Still, it seems there are few days when we're comfortably 'medium' busy. That surely must be the happy medium everyone refers to!

Rush. Rush. Rush. We're so busy being busy. So tired of being so tired. We feel overwhelmed and under-appreciated. No matter how well organised we are, and how efficient we are at time management, there never seem to be enough hours in the day. Most people I speak with share this thought.

In fact, time seems to have replaced caviar, champagne and Corvettes as the true luxury of our modern age. The phenomenal growth in service businesses is no surprise because any thing an organisation can do to save customers more time will be considered true value-adding and will be rewarded with increased business. After all, just look at the growth in domestic cleaning services, not to mention the fact that you can now even get someone in a mobile van to wash your dog. Or to walk it!

I must say that, apart from travel commitments, if you're too busy to walk your own dog, you're probably too busy! After all, what's the point of having a pooch in the first place if you're unable to spend time with it? Surely your role as an owner extends beyond working ridiculous hours just to buy bigger and better dog food? And the time you have available to spend with your pet is relative to the time you have for your family and friends. When I hear executives speak of spending qual-ity time with their children and they mean only 20 minutes once a day, I know it's time for them to reassess their priorities, even if they genuinely feel they're putting in the long hours for the benefit of the family.

The reality is that we'll never get more hours in a day, however much we may wish for them! Therefore, it's imperative to schedule the important things in our lives into our calendar before they get squeezed out with the other inevitable demands on our time. So think about what it is that you wish you had more time for. Then, for a month, schedule in your diary those 'appointments' with your family and yourself. Be sure to keep 95 per cent of those appointments as faithfully as you would a business commitment. This doesn't mean that your 'to do' list will get done any faster, but it does mean that you'll feel significantly less frustrated and resentful about never having any time for what you want to do, rather than simply being in response mode to everyone else's demands on your time.

Time is, after all, the most valuable asset we have in life and we can't make any more of it. I'm beginning to realise that no matter how many late nights and weekends I work, my 'to do' list will never get completely done. Despite faithfully following time management principles and prioritising it into A, B and C lists, it just seems to grow exponentially with all the things I could or should be doing, especially with creative new ideas.

After a serious illness, I suddenly found myself with too much time in the hospital, worrying about all the things I didn't have the time to do back at the office. When I returned to work, I felt even more swamped and after a frenzy of trying to catch up, realised I never would. The only option was to be more ruthless in setting priorities, to sub-contract out some work, and simply not do some jobs.

I've also learned to be a little gentler with myself. Rather than beat myself up at the end of the day for all the things which I didn't get done, I try to pat myself on the back for all the things that I *did* manage to get done in the day, both professionally and personally.

This minor form of self-congratulation doesn't mean I've caught up on my 'to do' list but I certainly have improved my daily 'to be' list. It's something I need to keep re-focusing on, especially during unusually busy times or after one of those inevitable events like a computer breakdown, burglary, flat tyre, illness or some other unexpected occurrence which throws even the best-laid daily plans out of balance. That's when we need to remind ourselves that any slavish return to an overwhelming 'to do' list must only be temporary and that our 'to be' list is more important because, after all, we're human beings—not humans doing.

You know your 'to do' list is out of control, when you've scheduled time for visits to the loo and don't get around to it!

That's why it seems ironic, possibly could even be considered hypocritical, that I did the final edit of this book on balance on a weekend! Does that

22

reflect on my credibility? Possibly, but in reality, there are always likely to be some times when our lives are temporarily out of balance in order to meet pressing deadlines. As long as it's only temporary, that's OK so there's little point in getting more stressed about those already stressful situations.

Whenever I'm feeling swamped with all the time pressures coming down on me and pointing a finger of blame at the pressures of our modern age, I try to remind myself of a time when we imagine such pressures weren't present. Nevertheless, Michelangelo was quoted as saying:

'Lord, grant that I may always desire more than I can accomplish.'

In many ways, that phrase can be symbolic of any individual striving for a full life, with enough dreams and personal projects to last beyond many lifetimes. We'll probably never get it all done, though, so don't worry because:

'The only person who got everything done by Friday was Robinson Crusoe.'

5

'The opportunity of a lifetime must be grasped within the lifetime of that opportunity.'

Roy Lea

How often do you hear people say that they could, should or would have done such and such if circumstances had been different at the time? Or lament that opportunities have just passed them by while others have been luckier?

Certainly, timing is important. If you were born after 1492, it would have been impossible to discover North America; or after 1969, unfeasible to be the first man on the moon. Still, in our everyday lives, hundreds—probably even thousands—of opportunities pass us by because we aren't ready to grasp them.

There's a proverbial story of two shoe salesmen sent to Africa 50 years ago. One reported to head office:

'All of the natives go barefoot so there is no market here for shoes.'

The other noted:

'All of the natives go barefoot, so there is a tremendous market for shoes.'

One saw a problem while the other saw an opportunity.

So too, as we're now well into the new millennium, many will see problems of downsizing, restructuring and increased global competition and feel powerless. Meanwhile, others will see a chance to turn a problem into an opportunity and start a business—possibly a line of work that didn't even exist before. The growth of home-based, service industry businesses is phenomenal, as evidenced by companies which provide dog grooming, massage and domestic help, not to mention the infinite opportunities on the Internet.

When those start-up businesses become successful, someone will inevitably say with envy:

'Gee they were lucky to be there at the right time and the right place.'

Timing certainly plays a part, but it is equally important to actually *implement* the ideas which you may be thinking about. One good idea implemented is worth a thousand which are simply talked about. It's great to dream big dreams, but we all know people who never do anything but daydream as the world passes them by. Many actually have excellent ideas but don't translate those thoughts into a plan of action to take advantage of the opportunity that they may see. They just talk, talk, talk.

Most of us are exposed to similar opportunities within our communities, but few people recognise them and an even smaller percentage take advantage of those opportunities, with only a handful actually following through with their plans.

This is especially true when the going gets tough and things don't go according to our original plan. My mother used to have an array of sayings such as:

'If you find yourself in hot water, take a bath'
'If life gives you lemons, make lemonade'
'If you sleep on it, it will seem better in the morning'

She'd also remind me, as a teenager, that opportunity knocks once but temptation rings on the doorbell! Even as adults, it's so easy to be tempted into activities that don't contribute to our long-term goal of seizing the opportunity presented. It's easy to get caught up with other activities that don't bring us any closer to our bigger goals.

We look at the use-by dates or shelf life of products on the supermarket shelves without realising that we too have expiry dates as human beings on this planet. It's easy to spot those people whose creativity has long since expired, their thoughts turned sour, their dreams dried up or their minds gone mouldy. Rather than truly living their lives and focusing on what they still *can* do, they lament their missed opportunities and complain about what they can't do anymore.

'If only I'd been as lucky as so and so . . .' they say, conveniently forgetting that luck is a four-letter word, spelled w.o.r.k. They tell anyone who will listen that they never got that lucky break or their timing was always bad.

Tom Peters is quoted, in his biography, as saying: 'Timing is a word that business persons by and large prefer to luck because it makes it sound as if you might have played at least a little role in the outcome.'

Timing is certainly a factor in many success stories. Often, the first party to bring an idea to market becomes the most successful. Some opportunities may be longlasting, while others are passing fads, which must be maximised within a short time frame. For example, if a city is hosting the Olympics, there is a relatively short window of opportunity for individual entrepreneurs to take advantage of the opportunities leading up to, during and immediately following the influx of tourists for the games. Yet there still remain longer-term opportunities in terms of developing infrastructures to leave a legacy.

I was brought up to believe that all people were created equal. As I've matured, I realise this childhood truism is not the case. All men and women are not created equal—physically, mentally, economically or in any other way. Yet all men and women should have equal opportunities to develop their own unique talents to the very best of their individual abilities, cognisant of the fact that:

'The opportunity of a lifetime must be grasped within the lifetime of that opportunity.'

6

'It's not the mountain we conquer, but ourselves.'

Sir Edmund Hillary

Few of us will ever have the desire to set as tough a challenge as conquering Mt Everest, but most of us do indeed set smaller personal challenges for ourselves along life's journey. Facing my fortieth birthday, I was determined to avoid a mid-life crisis and replace it with the experience of climbing the highest mountain in Africa, Mt Kilimanjaro, nearly 6000 metres high.

They say that life begins at 40, but when I commenced training, I was quite convinced that everything else began to wear out, spread out or fall out! As plans for the trip progressed, it occurred to me that I wasn't really the rugged outdoors type. In fact, my normal idea of roughing it was when room service was late at a luxury hotel! And as for the joy of sleeping under the stars, I definitely preferred the creature comforts of the five stars!

Nevertheless, planning and training continued for this challenge, which I couldn't quite explain to others. Everyone thought I should be satisfied to have a party and receive insulting birthday cards from well-meaning friends. But . . .

For a moment, picture yourself standing on top of the highest mountain in Africa. Dawn breaks on a crystal-clear morning as you breathe in the freshness of the rarified mountain air. You gaze down on the vastness of Kenya to one side and Tanzania on the other: 360-degree views over Africa as far as the eye can see. The sun bounces a beautiful pinkish-blue light off the icy glacier-like formations at the summit. It is a freak of nature for these peaks to be located at the equator. It was the most beautiful sight I had ever seen.

At the same time, imagine yourself shivering in minus-18 degree Celsius temperatures, feeling nauseous and battling a crashing headache from the altitude. You're gasping for air and hyperventilating. Then you see crosses where others have perished. I'd completed full marathons but never remember feeling as simultaneously elated and exhausted as I did during the final ascent of Kilimanjaro. Maybe it had something to do with the no pain—no gain theory.

We commenced the final climb in the middle of the night. The guide said that was to avoid avalanche danger when the sun hit the snow. But I think the real reason he woke us up in the middle of the night was because if we'd seen the full extent of what we had to do during daylight, we might not have done it! Isn't that the same with many projects we take on at work? If we knew how hard it might be, maybe we wouldn't volunteer. However, those who achieve more than others always do so.

It was sheer shale all the way up the mountain. It seemed that we took three steps forward and two steps back; three forward and two back; three forward and two back. Isn't it a bit like that at work as well? In fact, isn't it a bit like that in life? Just when we feel we're making progress, we sometimes slip back. But again, what separates winners from losers is that winners keep going forward and keep focused on their goal, even when they have temporary setbacks along the way.

Although I couldn't actually see the top of the mountain, I could picture it in my mind's eye and knew that's where I wanted to be. Yes, there were times during the night that I felt like giving up and turning back, but I kept visualising my goal and reminding myself that I hadn't come this far to quit, when I was so near but so far away.

It would have been more tempting to turn around if I'd succumbed to the feelings of doubt and the menacing avalanche of negativity that we so often let creep into our everyday lives. Often at work, I've felt that the learning curve was so steep that I should have had on safety ropes—and admittedly, there have been times when I didn't complete the project on the ground for whatever justification I could conjure up at the time. But I'm pleased that

30

I never lost sight of my goal when climbing Mt Kilimanjaro, by clearly keeping my focus on reaching the top.

Shortly afterwards, I had the privilege of meeting Sir Edmund Hillary at his home in New Zealand. I was in awe of the tall, well-built man, a childhood hero of mine. Although then well into his seventies, he had a larger than life presence and for an international icon, the first man on top of Everest, he was one of the most down-to-earth men I'd ever met.

'Just call me Ed,' the former beekeeper encouraged as I asked if he had visualised and always known he would be the first man on top of the world.

'No,' he replied. 'Of course, I had a goal. I wasn't just tramping around and found myself on top of Everest. I didn't know I would make it because there were so many uncertainties. But what's the point of having a goal if you know you're going to make it? What's the challenge in that?'

Thinking about that question, I realised the wisdom behind it. I also realised that we often don't set our personal goals high enough, settling instead for mediocrity. Around this time, I received a fax from Queensland mountaineer Michael Groom, indicating that one of his climbing partners, Tenzing's grandson, was interested in putting the first Australian female on top of Everest and would I be interested? Would I be interested! But I also realised that, as important as it is to set high goals for oneself, it's also important to feel that you're in as strong a position as possible to achieve them. I'd broken my sacrum only eight months earlier and doubted whether I could attain the required fitness and finance soon enough. I reluctantly reached this decision after exchanging more faxes and speaking with the New Zealand expedition leader, Rob Hall.

I intuitively didn't believe I had very good odds of succeeding on this occasion, and it was agreed that I would start training for the following expedition. Disappointed as I was, I had no idea that my earlier injury had been a blessing in disguise and was shocked and devastated to learn that Rob Hall and eleven others had perished in a freak storm on Everest on 10 May 1996.

His last words were to his wife in New Zealand, from a mobile phone at the summit. Mountaineering technology had certainly changed since Sir Edmund's ascent in 1953, but the determination of the individual to succeed against the unpredictability of the elements had not.

Technology continues to embrace new frontiers and there are always those pioneers at the forefront of discovery. Less than fourteen months after that fateful expedition, volcanoes were discovered on Mars—volcanoes that are three times the height of Everest!

About two weeks after Rob Hall perished, I received a postcard he had previously sent from base camp. As the world media analysed and debated the pros and cons of commercial expeditions, I just kept looking at his simple signature on the card and wondering how often we make mountains out of molehills, with relatively minor problems we encounter along the way in our everyday lives. I then realised that my broken sacrum, which was admittedly painful and debilitating, was only a molehill. It was a challenge that I certainly hadn't set for myself, but one that I nevertheless had to overcome at the time, with the help of doctors and friends.

I also realised that most people would never have any desire to risk their lives climbing a mountain, but we all have those figurative mountains in our everyday lives, sometimes seeming like insurmountable challenges looming large above us at the time. But, whether we're on a mountain or off, we still need to tackle those challenges in the same manner one climbs a mountain . . . one step at a time. When I'd climbed Kilimanjaro for my fortieth birthday, I realised that, unlike the cliché, life does not begin at 40. It begins the day we're born and it's not as important that we celebrate our actual birth dates than it is to take the time to celebrate the miracle of each and every day in between. Even on those days when we're trying to climb out of the depths of despair, Sir Edmund Hillary's words still ring true to those who never have any desire to climb a mountain because:

'It's not the mountain we conquer, but ourselves.'

7

'Everybody can be great because anybody can serve.'

Martin Luther King Jr

In terms of service to humankind, few of us will ever change the course of history to the degree that Martin Luther King did. Still, this great leader's words are a reminder that we can, indeed, all be of service to our country, clan, colleagues and customers.

Historically, in Western society, customer service jobs have been regarded as menial tasks. Someone worked in the service sector, waiting tables or pumping petrol, until they found a 'real' job.

Such roles had mistakenly been considered only as a means to an end, rather than worthwhile career paths in their own right. That paradigm has shifted considerably, and it is estimated that over 70 per cent of jobs are in the service sector. Thus there is an increased emphasis in all segments of the economy to dramatically improve customer service levels for increased competitive advantage. This transformation won't occur overnight, however, because of traditional beliefs of the nature of service.

The dictionary contains two quite different meanings for the word 'service'. One is 'the attendance of an inferior upon a superior'. This implies subservience, and few of us wish to be—or to be seen to be—subservient to anyone! Thus we rightly reject that notion of service.

Another definition states that service is 'the act of being useful'.

Surely we all want to be useful on this planet!

What a contrast between the two definitions! It's high time we discarded the first and wholeheartedly embraced the second. While subservience is considered lowly, surely being useful is one of the most highly acclaimed states to which we can aspire when serving customers.

On 29 September 1997, I heard the Dalai Lama speak to 10 000 people in the Sydney Entertainment Centre. He was later asked a question about the meaning of life—something we all ask ourselves from time to time. He smiled and simply responded:

'There are two meanings of life: to be happy and to be useful.'

Although I'm not sure that this answer adequately answered my own questions about the meaning of life, his comment certainly aroused my curiosity. On further investigation, I learned that such thoughts are not restricted to Buddhist beliefs. In fact, in the Bible, Jesus is quoted as saying:

'Those who wish to be great amongst you should also serve.'

Hindu, Muslim and Jewish friends inform me that there are similar teachings in their faiths and a former IBM colleague, now studying theology, assured me that the concept of being useful was an underlying theme in virtually every religion in the world.

I'm not advocating any particular religious base, but rather a general philosophy of being useful as individuals while we are on this planet. Since so much of our time is spent at work, it seems only sensible that employees approach their everyday tasks with the fundamental premise that they are in fact being useful to those they serve. This would result in a tremendous shift in customer satisfaction levels, rather than the all too frequent attitude of 'I just work here'. If all workers rejected this latter attitude, they would also be happier during their working hours. Even if they were employed at a job that they didn't see as their lifetime career, they could better enjoy their time on that task and make the best of every service situation, believing that they actually were being useful and making a contribution.

We cannot all be heroes
and thrill a hemisphere
With some great daring venture
Some deed that mocks at fear.
But we can fill a lifetime
with kindly acts and true

*There's always noble service
for noble souls to do.*

Margaret Miller Gallacher Smart

I knew her as Mum and long after her death, I found these words typed on now yellowed paper by a humble stenographer around the time Martin Luther King was born in 1929.

Apart from her friends, not many people have ever heard of Margaret Miller Gallacher Smart. She wasn't famous, apart from her cakes for church bake sales but she contributed in her own unique way nonetheless.

Conversely, few people have *not* heard of Martin Luther King and his tremendous contribution to civil liberties though few would be aware that he also said:

*If a man is called to be a street sweeper, he
should sweep streets even as Michelangelo painted
or Beethoven composed music or Shakespeare
wrote poetry. He should sweep streets so well that
all the host of heaven and earth will pause to say,
here lived a great sweeper who did his job well.*

King was undoubtedly right in more ways than one when he stated:

'Everybody can be great because anybody can serve.'

8

'It takes practice to turn common sense into common practice.'

Catherine DeVrye

Some wise old cowboy once commented that:

'Horse sense is something which horses have to stop 'em betting on people!'

That's because four-legged animal behaviour is somewhat more predictable than the two-legged kind! Yet, ironically, humans can also be predictable in their comments.

'I didn't learn anything I didn't already know. Isn't there anything new in management thinking today? It just seems too simple. Isn't it just common sense?'

Have you ever asked yourself such questions as you walked away from a business or personal development seminar? So why did you spend your hard-earned money and contribute, along with growing numbers of others, to making the speaking and training business such a high-growth industry in this millennium?

Having presented to audiences on five continents, you may be surprised to hear that I, too, ask this question of others and myself. In doing so, a few answers stand out.

Although we're looking for quick fixes and instant responses in this fast-paced, high-tech world, we also realise at a deeper level that there are no such readily available answers to the increasingly complex environment in which we live and work. Anyone who isn't somewhat confused in today's information age probably isn't well informed!

The latest electronic gadgetry, selling in cyberspace or sophisticated corporate strategic plans still don't solve the age-old fundamental problem of how to get employees to apply common sense—nor, importantly, how to turn such common sense into common practice.

Because, fundamentally, people are still people—with their strengths and weaknesses sometimes blatantly evident but often masked beneath a corporate cloud of intrigue and game playing.

After all, if everyone knew that the particular problem was so simple, maybe our job wouldn't be all that important. Worse still, maybe we wouldn't be all that important. So, we've been swept up by the latest management theories and can articulate the most recent buzzwords to impress peers, bosses, customers and subordinates—in fact, anyone willing to listen. But the gap remains between theory and reality. In our quest for virtual reality, we may often overlook the obvious, actual reality of a relatively simple solution.

We're so busy impressing that it's sometimes depressing! And, if we take the time to think about it—which we seldom do—so many of the buzzwords seem little more than shallow echoes of someone else's thoughts. Therefore, it is easier not to think too much and simply go along with whatever management style is in vogue. After all, if we had a completely clear desk, no phone ringing and simply sat in the office 'thinking', we'd soon be out of a job, having been incorrectly labelled as unproductive.

We've bought into the paradigm (oops—sorry—there's one of those unavoidable buzzwords) that it's more important to be busy being busy than it is to be busy being useful, making a meaningful contribution. That's why attending a seminar is in many ways a perfectly legitimate way of 'doing nothing' for an hour or a day. We can sit, listen and absorb what someone else says, without the usual pressure of meeting a deadline or an expected outcome for the day; taking time out and taking stock mentally.

I used to be flattered when clients would say:

'As a result of attending your seminar, we saved $300 000; or increased productivity 30 per cent.'

Now, although I am still pleased to hear such results, my ego has matured enough to know that it really wasn't what I *said*—but what *they heard*. More importantly, it was due to how they subsequently acted on the information they heard. What's more, it may not even have been the first time that they heard it, but it was possibly the first time it registered and struck a chord for them. They may have been too busy before to grasp the same message, now presented in a different way. All I— or any speaker—can do is to serve as a catalyst, by presenting material in a slightly different light, with a blend of humour and anecdotes to make that information relevant.

Basically, I see myself as a value-added re-packager of information services (oops—there's another buzzword, but as I said, that's what many of you still identify with!). It sounds more impressive than saying 'professional speaker'. After all, we're tired of the same over-the-top hype associated with speakers. Most audience members want to replace hype with hope—not a false hope, but a genuine belief that we, as individuals, can make a difference to our working environments and individual lives.

What we really want is a breath of fresh air for the brain! In today's information age, too many people are drowning in information but thirsting for knowledge and hoping for the occasional, refreshing sip of wisdom amidst the onslaught of letters, faxes, phone messages and now e-mails. We sometimes feel we need a gigantic snorkel since we're unlikely to keep our heads above the informational water line. As our world becomes more complicated, deep down inside we yearn for a return to greater simplicity, but are reluctant to admit it openly because simplicity implies a simpleton and we certainly wouldn't want anyone to label us as such!

I'll never forget a seminar I gave in Edinburgh in May 1997 to a predominantly male audience of 300, from the transport industry. As I commenced, most arms were defensively folded and the body language clearly implied: 'What's a woman from the colonies likely to tell us?'

By the time the hour was up, the same audience was visibly relaxed, laughing, talking, even participating—much to my relief. One burly truck driver approached me after and without mincing words, plainly stated:

'When you started, I thought that was a load of s___t! But, after a while, I realised you were on to something. You didn't actually tell me anything I didn't know, but let me tell you what you did.'

With that, he slammed his huge hand against the back of his skull. I looked at him quizzically and asked for further explanation. He again slammed the back of his head and simultaneously said:

'I knew a lot of that stuff before, but you moved it from the back of my brain to the front of my brain! And if I hadn't come today, I'd still be back at work, too busy to take time to think about it. I didn't want to come but I'm glad I did because you actually talked common sense and I'm going to put some of it into practice next week.'

I believe it's good to be a little sceptical and questioning while still being open to new thoughts— or old ones presented in new ways. Because it's entirely possible that the key to the future is to return to the simple truths of the past—back to the future where:

'It takes practice to turn common sense into common practice.'

9

'The man who swims against the stream knows the strength of it.'

Woodrow Wilson

This statement implies that life has to be a struggle, and I'm not saying that it isn't at times—nor that struggle does not build strength of character, which I believe it does. However, there comes a time when too much struggle only strangles. And aren't many of us guilty of using our limited energy reserves on tasks we're not good at, rather than going with the flow of our strengths? In surfing, it's imperative to learn to use the energy of the wave to propel you forward and then you don't need to paddle nearly as hard. You do need to paddle harder to catch one, but once you know what to do, the momentum will take you forward.

Panic is one of the most dangerous things for surfers and business owners. And relaxing is one of the toughest. Yet if you're being dumped in the surf, the best thing to do is relax, as it allows you to hold your breath longer under water. How many bankrupt businesses do you know whose owners panicked and drowned with debtors, rather than riding out a tough time?

I first learned to surf about the same time as I started my own business. Like all small businesses in the first few years of operation, it was struggling. And I was also struggling with my new, so-called recreational pursuit. I was extremely frustrated with surfing and was frankly getting quite despondent at my inability to catch a wave and stand up without getting dumped mercilessly under water. There I'd find myself gasping for air, churning around out of control beneath the waves like a limp rag in a washing machine, not knowing which way was up, struggling finally to the surface for a gulp of air before the next wave tossed me under again. In fact, it seemed a bit like my fledgling business. The harder I tried, the worse it got and I'd return to work feeling defeated, rather than energised, after a spell in the water.

What could I be doing wrong? I'd taken lessons from a good coach, read a book, practised, watched others and technically knew exactly what to do. So why couldn't I surf? Were there other lessons that weren't in the book—lessons equally applicable to business?

The hardest one for me was to learn to wait quietly and patiently for just the right wave for my skill level. Patience is a word I hadn't heard in business life, as we were always told to go out and create new business and not wait for it to come to us. That's exactly what I'd been doing in my own business. I'm not suggesting that anyone should sit in the office and wait for the phone to ring, but there are many situations where frantic activity actually doesn't make any difference whatsoever to the bottom line, as timing is all wrong for reasons beyond the control of the proprietor.

Timing is everything in surfing as well. An average good ride on a wave lasts only a matter of seconds, so it's important to be in the moment. One of the great things about surfing is that you don't have any choice but to be in the moment and your mind is magnificently clear of any distractions. You simply enjoy the pure joy of the ride before going for the next one. It is not always easy going, but it is important to have fun. That's what surfing and work should be about. It's certainly a foreign concept to the one I was accustomed to in the corporate world: being involved in frantic activity and rushing on to the next project before savouring the success of the past one.

Obviously, balance is important to be able to stand on a surfboard. It's equally vital to have in your business life. Because what's the point if you don't enjoy the ride! How many people do you know who never take time out to enjoy riding the waves of their success? They constantly feel as if an imaginary tidal wave of trouble is about to again drown them in the depths of despair, as they get caught up with their nagging negative thoughts?

A life without positive energy is like an ocean without waves. A life without hope is like a seagull without wings. And a life without joy is like surf without sound.

In the ocean, it's important to be able to understand rip tides. One of the first things you learn is that if you get caught in a rip, dragging you out to sea, it is important not to fight against it but wait until it ends, as they don't go on forever. Then paddle back towards shore. In fact, experienced surfers always paddle out with a rip. It's an example of using something as frightening as a rip to your advantage.

The same rule applies to the flow of the economy, which may be going against you. That's not to say you succumb and admit defeat, feeling that you can't do anything but be sucked out by the monetary tide. But, by being more of an astute observer, versus frantic, futile activity for the sake of activity, it will be to your advantage if you don't use up valuable energy fighting the tide of events in the economic world that you are powerless to control. Sometimes trying harder makes absolutely no difference at all and it's important to have the wisdom to know when enough is enough and to go with the flow, recognising that Woodrow Wilson was correct in stating that:

'The man who swims against the stream knows the strength of it.'

10

'The world expects results. Don't tell them about the labour pains. Show them the baby.'

Anon

Think of all the excuses you've heard for why results haven't been achieved. Think of all the times that someone has delivered a product or service but expects you to listen to their story of the difficulties it took to deliver simply what they said they would. Now, think of those people who always cheerfully provide what they promised, when they promised, as they promised. Who would you rather do business with? Who would you rather be friends with? Someone who is usually reliable or someone who's not?

Woody Allen once said that 'Half of success is just showing up'. I would like to add . . . 'when you said you would!' My cleaner has done so dependably for over a decade and I value her reliability as much as her scrubbing skills.

At least mobile phones now give trades-people and others providing goods or services the ability to call if they're unavoidably detained on a previous job. Surely doctors and airline offices could also call most patients and passengers to inform them of delays beyond the control of the organisation, thus giving the customer the opportunity to re-schedule or arrive a little later. Most customers appreciate the fact that an airline can't do anything about delays due to bad weather and understand if a doctor is caught up in an emergency operation. What they won't tolerate are continual delays due to overbooking or poor planning on the part of the supplier.

If the occasional delay does occur, they appreciate a very brief explanation but expect the supplier to focus on the customer's reason for doing business. We get tired of individuals and organisations that continually make excuses—blaming their staff, suppliers, the government or the man on the moon for their shortcomings.

Time is life. And I've no intention of wasting mine listening to some long-winded explanation as to why a business promise hasn't been fulfilled. I'm often tempted to hand the person some loose change and say: 'Go find a pay phone and call someone who cares!'

Unfortunately, some businesses still insist on adopting the 'martyr mentality' as their *modus operandi*. Recovery stories are legendary and often impressive, but to be honest, I'm not at all impressed by the fact that someone walked barefoot in the snow for 20 kilometres to deliver the goods if they could easily have done the same thing in comfort by spending more time pre-planning in the first place. It's also better to say no nicely, rather than over-promise and under-deliver.

Of course, there's also the danger of spending so much time on the planning phase that you never get around to the action phase! This is often true of those individuals who are constantly telling you what they're 'gonna do'. Years later, you're still hearing the same thing but seeing no results.

In May 1998, I had the honour of speaking to 1100 Hewlett Packard female engineering staff in Fort Collins and sharing the platform with a woman in her late seventies. Kathryn Hach-Darrow, CEO of Hach Chemical Company and winner of the Colorado Woman of the Year Award, was asked how much time she spent on her strategic plan and mission statement in the development stage of her now multi-million dollar business. This sprightly grandmother, who had started the venture with her husband nearly half a century earlier, replied:

'We didn't have strategic plans or mission statements in those days and my goal was very simply to keep the wolf from the door as the stork was flying in the window!'

With such a practical approach, no wonder her business had thrived. A working mum long before it was commonly acceptable to be so, she intuitively knew that:

'The world expects results. Don't tell them about the labour pains. Show them the baby.'

11

'You can't drive into the future if you're looking into a rear vision mirror.'

Anon

With rapid change so prominent in today's world, too many people look back on the 'good old days', recalling less complicated times. Reminiscing can certainly be pleasant, but it's futile to long for a return to the past, rather than looking forward to the future.

Even with all the turmoil in the world today, it's worth remembering that we should enjoy the present because, in a few years, these times will become *our* 'good old days'.

We must look forward, not back. Canadian by birth, ice hockey runs in my veins and I love the story about an interview with Wayne Gretsky's father. 'Why,' asked the journalist, 'is your son the #1 player in the world? How is he so great in always knowing where the puck is?'

Gretsky senior replied: 'He's not great because

he knows where the puck is. He's great because he knows where it's *going.*'

Unlike even the best of ageing hockey players, the pace of change is unlikely to slow down. On the contrary, it's likely to accelerate faster than a vehicle on the Grand Prix circuit. Undoubtedly, these changes can cause stress, just as the drivers of such racing cars experience stress.

When the Grand Prix was held in Adelaide, in South Australia, physiologists conducted a study on the stress levels of the drivers. Electrodes were attached to their hearts to ascertain when they experienced the highest stress levels. Was it when they risked their lives at 300 kilometres per hour, racing down the straight? Was it when they turned left or right? Was it when another driver was nearby? The researchers were surprised to find that none of these life-threatening conditions produced the most stress. In fact, the highest recorded levels of stress were when the drivers were safely at a pit stop. This initially seemed surprising but, on analysis, made perfect sense because at that point in time someone *else* had control over their vehicles!

How often do we feel 'in the pits' and under stress when we sense—rightly or wrongly—that someone else has control over our lives; when we feel powerless ourselves, but have to stand by and watch? Often, we may think we have no control when in fact there are many more options for action than we may imagine.

As Henry Ford once said:

'Whether you think you can or think you can't, you're probably right.'

It's important to never forget that, as individuals, we must take control of our lives. It's easy to forget this in times of rapid change. It's equally important to remember that many changes are for the better, not the worse. Yet we seldom hear anyone lamenting those changes for the good. Some readily complain about a higher utility bill than 'what it used to be', but I've never heard anyone longing for the good old days when we didn't even have electricity or running water!

I recently spoke at an automotive conference and learned the astonishing fact that any car built since 1992 contains more sophisticated technology than the lunar space ship that landed on the moon in 1969! A single Pentium chip now has more computing power than that available to NASA during the entire research and development phases of the space program.

Astronaut John Glen provided a wonderful example of not looking backwards when, in November 1998 at age 77, he again circled the globe as he had first done in 1962—only in a more sophisticated craft. When I mentioned these remarkable facts to a friend, she replied:

'Yes, it is amazing. We've put one man on the moon . . . why can't we put them all there!'

I had to remind her that, even though she'd had a messy divorce, she hadn't always felt that way about her ex-husband, and it wouldn't do her any good to be bitter towards all men because, whether in our personal or professional lives . . .

'You can't drive into the future if you're looking into a rear vision mirror.'

12

'The best customer relations is not to treat your customers like you treat your relations.'

Catherine DeVrye

At first glance, you might think this quote is the antithesis of the truth. You may believe that any caring human being would, in fact, treat their relations as the most valuable asset in the world—with the utmost dignity and respect.

Yet how often is the reverse the case? If you think I'm being too harsh or cynical, just remember last Christmas when you felt swamped by family obligations. What percentage of time do we spend treating our relatives like the precious gold that we should, compared with the number of times we feel they're people we have to put up with or people we take for granted . . . until it's too late?

It's the same with our customers. Too often, we feel that our most valuable customers will always be there, as we frantically pour most of our efforts into chasing new business. Yet research shows that it costs five times more to obtain a new customer than to retain an existing one.

Too frequently, we see customers as people we must put up with or interruptions to a day filled with the busy pace of 'doing our job'. Think of the number of times you've been in a shop and the salesperson is more concerned about stocking the shelves, filling in an order form or talking to a supplier on the phone than about serving you. After all, the other things are measurable tasks that must be completed during their working day, or they may have to stay back late. They probably have a set number of these tasks on their 'to do' list and the last thing they need is another interruption in the form of a living, breathing customer.

Yet these interruptions are the reason that the business exists in the first place. Neither the manager nor accountant pays staff salaries. Although they may physically write the cheque, it's the accumulation of individual customers that actually pays the salary of each and every employee, from apprentices to executives.

Remember this the next time a customer 'interrupts' your day. Unlike your relatives, don't take them for granted or feel they're someone who needs to be tolerated. In short, don't treat your customers like you treat your relations. In fact, don't even treat your relations like you treat your relations! Make a point of telling them that you care about them—even that you love them. Admittedly, love isn't a word much mentioned in a business context, but if you're not happy at home, some of that emotion will inevitably be conveyed to your customers.

You may say that there's no need to tell your friends and family that you love them. You assume they'll know, just like the new groom who tells his wife on their wedding day: 'I love you. But don't expect me to say so every day. If it changes, I'll let you know!'

To avoid any accusations of being sexist towards men, I must confess that I've done likewise. I grew up in a family where we weren't demonstrative of our feelings and I'd never told my father how much I loved him, until it was too late and he lay unconscious in a coma.

I've made a lot of mistakes in my life and like to think I learn from them and don't repeat the same one twice. But I'll never have an opportunity to rectify that error. I encourage others not to make the same mistake. CEOs of major corporations have called me in near tears when their fathers passed away to thank me for reminding them of this. They didn't call because they didn't have close family who loved them dearly but possibly because as head of a company and a family, they felt they needed to be strong for those who relied on them. These were successful and caring men in both their professional and personal lives who recognised the importance of family and knew that:

'The best customer relations is not to treat your customers like you treat your relations.'

13

'Every day above the ground is a good one.'

Frank Jansen

It's been over a quarter of a century since I first heard this phrase from a wise old man. In his late seventies at the time, Frank Jansen was a truly great Australian—not a famous one . . . at least not beyond the boundaries of the Flemington Bowls Club. Frank wasn't a CEO or management guru but an average blue-collar working man who, through his own labour, combined with that of many others, formed the backbone of the great land down under.

I'd arrived in Australia with a backpack and $200, following the sudden death of my parents soon after I'd graduated from university in the USA. I'd previously thought the world was my oyster. Suddenly, it was shattered like a semi-trailer would a shell.

It was safe to say that my life was at an all-time low when I had the good fortune to meet Frank. His simple homespun philosophy reminded me that, regardless of tragedy, which strikes all of us sooner or later, every day above the ground truly is a good one.

Yet how often do we take this for granted? How often do we worry about little annoyances that upset our plans? How often do we forget to give thanks for all that we do have, rather than lamenting that which we do not; lose sleep over the little things; vent anger at those who may be closest to us? In other words, how often do we lose perspective?

And, more importantly, how can we re-gain it?

Simply take a deep breath and ask yourself an important question:

'In 100 years, will this really matter?' In 100 days? Or even 100 hours? Tell yourself out loud, if you must:

'This is all relative.'

It could be relative to starving children in Africa, war ravaging some far-flung part of the globe or, more likely, simply relative to other events which occur in our own small corner of the world—relative in terms of our own life plan and families, friends and health.

After all, it's seldom the tragedies that ruin our day. It's the jammed photocopier, the phone company which made a mistake on our statement, a teenage son who dented the car, office politics, the mobile phone which dropped out of range, a lost computer document without backup, a missed wake-up call or a late flight. The list goes on.

Frank Jansen also told me that when we humans come off the production line, we arrive without any instructions on how to live life and certainly without any lifetime guarantees.

'Y'know Cath, it's not only a car which can be recalled by its maker and you never know when that might be.'

As I was learning to drive on the other side of the road at the time, I wondered if it might be sooner than later! But, every day since, I've realised that we're all surrounded with reminders of Frank's philosophy but usually don't see or hear the wisdom of his words until something close to home is affected. And we become so blasé about car accidents or obituary notices until it's someone we know.

On 30 July 1997, a freak landslide buried 18 people at Thredbo ski resort. Few Australians will ever forget the long wait and the horror of pulling bodies from the rubble. One victim was a friend of mine who had lived life to the fullest. It was hard to imagine anyone, let alone Wendy O'Donohue, buried alive. It was another all too poignant reminder that every day above the ground is a good one.

Meanwhile, how many people don't really live their lives to the full? They go about their daily existence in mechanical fashion, while actually buried in the depths of their own self-despair? You know the types—no matter what they have, they're never satisfied. The grass is too green, the sky is too blue, the ice cream is too cold: full of enough negativity to sink the *Titanic*.

Admittedly, we all harbour negative thoughts from time to time. When I was diagnosed with a malignant melanoma, the same disease that had killed my mother, I was feeling decidedly sorry for myself. Although I knew intellectually that negative thoughts would only contribute further to ill-health, I was an emotional wreck. I doubted the doctors' reassurance that they had 'got it all' and imagined myself suffering as my mother had a quarter of a century earlier. I then realised that the words Frank had used to comfort me then were just as relevant, if not more so, 25 years later.

Every morning when I wake up, and again last thing before I close my eyes at night, I say a silent thank you to no one in particular. Sleep is a marvellous healer combined with my personal daily reminder that:

'Every day above the ground is a good one.'

14

'Change is inevitable. Learning from change is optional.'

Catherine DeVrye

Do you sometimes feel that you're constantly banging your head against a wall only because it feels so good when you stop? Do you know people who, when faced with immovable objects, tasks or situations, never seem to stop banging their head against whatever imaginary brick wall is in their way? They never seem to learn. They never seem willing to adapt by looking at alternatives such as going around the brick wall rather than trying in vain to go through it.

It may be something as simple as a detour on a familiar, well-travelled road. I know a person who became incensed when repairs were being done to a street and they could no longer take their chosen route to work. One of his colleagues pointed out that she had inadvertently discovered that the alternative route was, in fact, shorter and contained one less set of traffic lights, so she would continue using it, even once repairs to the old route were completed. Still, our complainer complained, becoming almost obsessed with the diversion and how the change in route had changed his routine.

This same person was always the one whinging at work as well, resisting new technology, an altered product line, a new manager or renovations to the office layout. You name it, he resisted it, either actively or passively. Sometimes the grumble would be only a low mumble; at other times, the gripe would continue long after everyone else had forgotten there had even been a change! It wasn't hard to see why this employee, who was highly qualified and technically competent, had been passed over for promotions. As his manager at the time, I felt obliged to point this out during a performance review.

I cited a joke about two guys who went to see *True Grit*. John Wayne, who never falls off his horse, did so in that movie. One of the men had seen it before, so he bet his buddy five dollars that John Wayne would fall off his horse. Naturally, his friend took the bet.

After they came out of the picture theatre, he reached into his pocket to pay his bet, muttering that he couldn't believe that John Wayne fell off his horse. His friend refused to accept his winnings, admitting that he'd seen the movie before and had tricked his friend into the bet. The other replied: 'Well, I'd seen it before too, but I couldn't believe he'd fall off twice!'

I thought this story was a light-hearted example about optional learning from changed circumstances. However, the analogy seemed to fall on deaf ears when it came to the problem employee, which prompted me to reflect that you could lead a horse to water but you couldn't make it drink! The only drinking this dud ever did was at the pub; a thirst for knowledge seemed nonexistent because he was as stubborn as a mule and didn't have the horse sense to see that his days in the organisation were numbered if his negative attitude continued.

Few of us welcome all changes. All of us make mistakes. But one of the biggest mistakes of all is to welcome no change whatsoever. With the advent of cars in the nineteenth century, it was inevitable that there would be a decline in the buggy whip market. Computers have replaced typewriters. Faxes have replaced telegrams and are likely to become obsolete themselves with the growth in electronic mail.

In the 1950s, IBM founder Thomas Watson stated that there would only be a global market for five computers! In the 1970s, the chairman of Digital boldly declared that there would never be computers in the home. Later, the founder of Microsoft, Bill Gates, stated that no user would require more than 640K of memory! Even these leaders of multinational corporations hadn't anticipated the changes in the technology market at the time. What made their organisations successful under their leadership was their ability to admit their predictions were wrong and revise their strategies accordingly in a changing world.

Unlike the employee who refused to learn from change, these three men and countless other successful individuals had the horse sense—the common sense—to learn from the past to create a profitable future. They knew that change is a constant of any business.

Like the cowboy philosopher, Will Rogers, they also knew that even if you're on the right track, you'll get run over if you just stand there. Without doubt, they knew that:

'Change is inevitable. Learning from change is optional.'

15

'We must add meaning to our life or it will remain forever meaningless.'

Catherine DeVrye

Most authors hate the blank page. I love the blank page. It's a bit like life itself. On it, I can write whatever I want, create the reality I wish, fill it with whatever thoughts I want and even whatever actions I desire. I can leave it blank and admire its nothingness. Or I can become frustrated for the exact same reason. The choice of what I do is entirely mine.

I can use a pen or a keyboard to write fact or fiction. I can regurgitate research or implore my own imagination. I can write prose or poetry, and even put the words to music. These words can heal or harm. They can make others laugh or cry. I can write a letter or a contract, a receipt or a recipe, a biography or a brochure.

I can share how I've chosen to rearrange the 26 letters of the English alphabet or keep my writings to myself. I can toss the page in the fire or hit the delete key. The range and power of these choices, in print or in our daily lives, seems as endless as the blank page itself. Yes, I love the blank page. It's a blank life that I'd hate.

William Shakespeare once said that 'Nothing comes from nothing'. In some ways, each new day is like a blank piece of paper or computer screen waiting for us to create something from nothing; a blank canvas waiting to be filled with bleak gray or vibrant colour. We are the artists of our lives and should never forget that it's up to us to create, in the human form, a unique individual masterpiece that we're proud to call our own, thus showing the world our true selves. Few of us will ever be a Michelangelo or a Picasso, but each of us still has the talent to design a life with inner beauty as we define it.

As children, we probably did some amateur finger-painting without considering that each of us is as unique as our fingerprints. We probably were encouraged to colour inside the lines of our colouring books without realising that we sometimes need to go outside traditional boundaries to add new dimensions and colour to our lives. We probably filled our colouring books and our lives only with primary colours before we discovered the beauty of the many combinations and shades in between.

We'd gaze at the beauty of a rainbow without stopping to think that the colours signalling the end of a storm last only a few seconds. We must likewise colour our own lives with a rainbow on the horizon of hope, recognising that every cloud does indeed have a silver lining and, without the rain, we could never appreciate the rainbow. Is there really a pot of gold at the end of the rainbow? Or, isn't it more likely the hope of a brighter time after the storm? Such hope is the most important currency we carry, not in our wallets but in our hearts.

Helen Keller never read a book, or saw a painting or rainbow but, although blind since birth, she still knew that, even without seeing a glorious prism, it's impossible to remain a prisoner of despair if you colour your life with a rainbow of hope. She chose to do so, saying that 'Life is either a daring adventure or nothing.'

Although overcoming what many of us would have seen as overwhelming odds, facing a life without reading or rainbows, she knew that she could still write her own story and paint a life that was nothing short of a masterpiece. She rejected a life of nothingness and lived a life of daring adventure, meeting obstacles head-on and knowing the truth in the words:

'We must add meaning to our life or it will remain forever meaningless.'

16

'It's not what it costs to learn but what it costs to not learn.'

Catherine DeVrye

No matter how begrudgingly parents may complain about school fees and the price of books and equipment, they understand that these things are an investment in the future of their children. They know that a good education is something that, once gained, can never be lost through carelessness or theft.

As adults, many of us lament the times we didn't fully appreciate the value of that education and wasted time in class. Possibly, we didn't believe the education was relevant and, in some instances, we were right. Most of us never dreamed that we'd be going back to school, attending refresher courses, retraining for a new career or simply keeping up with the ever-changing knowledge developments in our chosen field. Even if someone had suggested that our education would be a lifelong pursuit, we probably would have ignored them, thinking we'd leave textbooks behind on graduation day.

No one ever told us that employers would require and sometimes supply ongoing education, or encourage us to undertake additional studies at our own expense just to stay competitive in the employment marketplace. Employers themselves would look at the bottom line and lament the amount of funds spent on staff training, wondering where savings could be made. In tough economic times, the training budget would often be the first to be cut, only to see a resultant shortage in necessary skills for the organisation to remain competitive down the track.

Smart businesses, large and small, see training not as an expense but as an investment. Tom O'Toole, owner of the very successful Beechworth Bakery in central Victoria, is often asked how a small country bakery can afford to train staff, many of whom are casual employees.

'What if you spend that money to train them, Tom, and they leave?'

'Yeah,' replies Tom dryly, 'but what if I don't train 'em—and they stay!'

Tom has never been to university, but has acquired a lifetime of knowledge in the school of common sense and applies the same principle as that espoused by the former President of Harvard University, Derek Bok, who was quoted as saying:

'If you think education is expensive, try ignorance.'

If it's true that ignorance is bliss, one can only

wonder why there aren't more happy people in the world! Tom may have left formal schooling at an early age but, like many successful men and women, he's certainly not ignorant and has taken responsibility for his own self-education by reading books, listening to tapes and attending seminars. He knows the wisdom in the words of Mark Twain, who said:

'A man who does not read good books has no advantage over the man who can't read them.'

Or Marshall McLuhan, who tells us that:

'The future of work consists of learning a living.'

A golfing friend of mine is a recently retired school principal but has no intention of retiring from a life of learning and enrolled in a computer course to keep her mind active. She commented as we strolled down the fairway:

'You know, it's quite frustrating to be a student and not a teacher after all these years and I now have a much better appreciation of people who may have learning difficulties. In fact, I think all teachers should periodically be required to take courses in subject areas *outside* their area of expertise so they can more fully appreciate the struggle others may have.'

We agreed that, like golf, many things look easy until you try them!

We also concurred that Francis Bacon may have been right when he said centuries earlier that 'Knowledge is power' but one also needs to know how to practically apply that knowledge and even reading the best golfing books in the world wasn't going to do anything for my slice!

In this day and age, when we're swamped with information, it's important to be able to sift useful information from the mass of useless data presented to us. Only if you can do that, do you have a chance to acquire the knowledge which is the source of that power. The better you can integrate knowledge from other sources within your practical life experiences, the greater your own personal supply of wisdom becomes. Not unlike Darwin's theory of survival of the fittest, the twenty-second century will inevitably be one of survival of the wisest. The people and experiences we encounter, whether positive or negative, all teach us something, even though the lesson may not be evident at the time. That knowledge and experience you've gained throughout the years is a priceless gift. Use it wisely and remember that, although you have paid a price to get to where you are today, and will likely continue to do so in the future . . .

'It's not what it costs to learn but what it costs to not learn.'

17

'If you don't think a customer is important, just trying doing without one for 60 days.'

Catherine DeVrye

Many individuals within large organisations pay lip service to customer service. They mistakenly think that the computer, the pay office or their boss generates their salary. They don't fully comprehend that their salaries are, in fact, paid by the sum total of the many and varied individual customers who chose to do business with that organisation.

We all can recall occasions when, as customers ourselves, we have felt as if we were treated as an interruption to an organisation's business, rather than the sole reason for the business to exist in the first place. Owner-operators of smaller ventures have a much greater appreciation of this often-overlooked fact of business life.

That's not to say that employees in large organisations don't increasingly recognise the importance of customer service. However, as their weekly or monthly wages aren't dependent on cash flow, they don't fully appreciate the significance of each and every customer transaction, no matter how small it may be. 'Someone' in the accounts receivable section will chase late payments while management worries about a decrease in revenue or reduced trade. They may even disclose financial results to staff, or offer a profit share plan to encourage everyone to do their best to increase sales and reduce costs. Employees may well grumble about budget cuts, but seldom are their personal lifestyles impacted by issues of cash flow, until things become so grim that layoffs are required. Thirty, 60 or 90-day terms of credit are not usually topics for discussion in the company cafeteria!

I know this to be true because I've been employed by the multinational IBM and an Australian government department, and now run my own small business which is a marked contrast to the public and private sector bureaucracies for which I once worked. There are pros and cons to both, as I soon discovered when I first started out. Although I loved the independence of being my own boss, I'd been blissfully cocooned from cash flow in the larger organisations, (although managing multi-million dollar budgets).

I was committed to delivering great customer service and worked for months to put together my first full-fee presentation as a professional speaker. By the time it was finished, I was both exhausted and exhilarated at the overwhelmingly positive response.

A couple of days later, I left for an extended holiday. On return, I was surprised that no cheque from the client had arrived. I wondered if I'd misjudged their reaction and maybe they had second thoughts about the benefit of my presentation since I'd offered a money-back guarantee. I mentioned this to a friend who had run her own business for some time.

'What was the date of the invoice?' she asked.

'What invoice? They laughed. They clapped. They'll send money.'

I was embarrassed by my naiveté. And, sure enough, within a week or so of mailing the invoice, a cheque arrived. I'd remembered the importance of satisfying the customer but had overlooked some of the basic mechanics of being rewarded for it.

I can now joke at my own expense about this lack of basic financial knowledge, but it's certainly no laughing matter when so often the reverse occurs and the process for payment is in place without first ensuring that the customer is satisfied! Too often people in organisations mistakenly believe that their procedures are more important than their customers.

In the many presentations I've given around the globe, I've espoused this important facet of customer service, but never did the words take on greater meaning than during a trip to Alaska where I'd spoken on a cruise conference. It was mid-May when we docked in Juneau. The sun was shining and the snow-capped mountains reflected in the sparkling clear blue water. In spite of the northern latitude, tourists enthusiastically disembarked from the ship in t-shirts.

We were greeted by the usual array of tour operators, never pushy and always friendly. But if tour operators weren't friendly, who would be, I thought. The whale-watching trip was magnificent, with sightings of both killer and humpback whales on either side of the smaller boat we had boarded. Naturally, most visitors were in an exuberant mood to later wander around and shop. Without exception, I noted the helpfulness and genuine warmth of the front line staff in both the shops and restaurants.

In one shop, I waited while a customer verbally abused one of the staff over what seemed to me a petty problem. I was impressed by how the sales assistant handled the complaint and then cheerfully turned to me as if nothing had happened. I commented on her complaint-handling ability and said how impressed I was by everyone's approach to customer service; unlike some city stores, everyone seemed genuinely glad to have the place full of bargaining tourists.

'Of course we're glad to see you. You're the first customers we've had in six months!' she laughed. 'The ice closes the waterway for much of the year.'

I asked whether that meant I could expect everyone to have a totally different attitude and be grumpy at the end of the season. She laughed again and remarked:

'You don't need to worry about that. Admittedly, we can be a little tired by then, but we know that when the last ship leaves for the season, it takes with it a precious cargo of customers.'

Yes, in Alaska they fully comprehend that:

'If you don't think a customer is important, just trying doing without one for 60 days.' (Or in their case, 180!)

18

'We all live under the same sky but we don't share the same horizon.'

Anon

Remember as a child how you would lie on your back, gaze lazily at the clouds and spot imaginary shapes floating by?

'That one looks like a horse,' you'd exclaim. 'And there's a spaceship.'

Sometimes your friend would readily see the same shape emerging. At other times, only your eyes would appreciate the ethereal image. Cloud formations change by the second and, as in a working environment, many people don't see opportunities until they have long since vanished into thin air. That's why there's usually a key competitive advantage in being first to the marketplace with a particular good or service.

With world trade, it's the same sun in the sky but the intensity of both light and competition differs from time to time and place to place. At night, the one moon beams down wherever we may be. The formation of the stars differs somewhat according to which hemisphere we view them from, but basically we all do live under the same sky, and it's not just pollution that prevents us from sharing the same horizon. There are differences in cultures and climates; economics and environments; politics and population densities; religions and rituals.

Most of us are too busy leading our own lives in our own small part of the world to give much thought to perspectives that others might share, and too busy to spend much time gazing towards the heavens. We're peering at a computer screen or watching the traffic. But, every now and then, an event prompts us to look skyward with a temporary resurgence of that childlike curiosity.

It's 18 November 1998 and a radio announcer encourages listeners to set their alarms for 4.00 a.m. to see brilliant flashes in the pre-dawn sky as balls of flame whiz across the horizon. Are they UFOs? Comets? A scientist on the talk show says it's the most spectacular meteorite shower in over three decades.

In fact, these harmless meteorites, which terrified our ancestors, are probably only the size of a football. And the bright glare which seems looming large on the horizon isn't the actual object glowing, but the vapour trail left in its path, which makes the meteorite appear much larger than it actually is. We learn that these meteorites travel at approximately 108 000 kilometres per hour, faster than a speeding bullet.

The scientist goes on to patiently explain that there are thousands of such meteorites falling all the time but they're seldom noticed because of daylight or pollution in our urban skies—and because, frankly, few people spend time gazing heavenward.

He explains that it's exactly the same principle as a falling star, which is much more readily spotted in a rural environment on a clear night. In fact, a falling star is no bigger than a grain of sand. But, again because of the speed at which it is travelling, it looks larger and it's not the heat of the object that is visible, but the heat generated from the speed at which it is travelling.

My amateur interpretation of the explanation made me think that there are similarities between meteorites and humans. It's not just the physical presence or size of the person you see at any particular moment in time, but—much more importantly—the trail they leave behind that makes the biggest impact. Some leave chaos and destruction—both physical and emotional—in their wake, while others leave lasting legacies. This is true whether the person is in the public limelight or an ordinary family member who still has the capacity to make a positive or negative impact on all those in their path.

We need to learn what information to accept and what to question. Tell a man that there are 400 billion stars and he'll believe you, but tell him that there is wet paint on a fence and he usually has to touch it!

Unlike meteorites, we need not aspire to travel at 108 000 kilometres per hour! But sometimes we do need to aim for the moon to be a star; to shine in our chosen area of endeavour. I remember, as a little girl, listening to Jiminy Cricket close each Walt Disney program with the words:

'When you wish upon a star, your dreams come true.'

Walt Disney had a dream that he followed in spite of numerous setbacks along the way. The opportunities were there for others to found theme parks or multi-billion dollar entertainment empires, but it was Disney who was the first successful pioneer, just as surely as Neil Armstrong was the first man on the moon. When you think of the billions of stars and people, it could have been someone other than Walt Disney or Neil Armstrong who had their names recorded in the history books.

Not everyone remembers the first lunar landing in 1969, but most people are still fascinated by the frontiers of outer space. So, what about that space between our ears? We need to use that important grey matter to ask how we can expand our personal horizons, how we can shine and light up, if not the world, at least the lives of some others. Like the childhood song, we need to discover what it is that makes us twinkle. With apologies to whoever wrote that first song, I've modified words, sung to the familiar tune:

Thinking, thinking little stars
Sometimes wondering who we are
Sometimes sad and sometimes bright
Turning darkness into light.
Twinkle, twinkle we're all stars
So unique in who we are!

It's that uniqueness which explains why:

'We all live under the same sky but don't share the same horizon.'

19

'If you travel a path with no obstacles, it probably doesn't lead anywhere.'

Catherine DeVrye

As adults, we've been on our chosen path for some time now and have met with inevitable obstacles—obstacles that even a genius couldn't have foreseen when we were born.

Most of us weren't born geniuses, but from childhood were tested for our IQ. We may have been accepted into Mensa or, alternatively, been disappointed at the results. Some people debate the socio-economic validity of such tests, while others point with glee to those so-called clever individuals who seem to have led tragic lives. Nevertheless, our Intelligence Quotient, better known simply as our IQ, became a recognised measure of brainpower—though not necessarily of success.

This isn't surprising considering the many other factors that influence our quest for success. Our PQ is just as important as our IQ. I refer here to the Persistence Quotient.

When I was a child, my mother always told me to 'watch my Ps and Qs'. I had no idea what she was talking about, although I knew perfectly well what she meant! So I've defined my own meaning for Ps and Qs as the Persistence Quotient. And we must indeed watch that we do persist in following our dreams or we'll find, like childhood, they'll slip away.

Few could argue that Thomas Edison would have possessed an extraordinary IQ. With hundreds of patents to his credit, the inventor of the light bulb also knew the importance of a high PQ. Without his Persistence Quotient, many inventions would have remained in darkness.

Edison was apparently interviewed when he was still struggling to perfect the light bulb. A young reporter asked:

'I understand that you have had thousands of failed experiments. How do you feel about so many failures with this concept of the light bulb, Mr Edison?'

'Ah,' the scientist replied, 'you're too young to understand that I haven't had 9999 failures. I may have had that many experiments but it simply means that I'm getting ever closer to finding the right solution, by ruling out 9999 that won't work.'

Whether this account of the interview is 100 per cent correct is irrelevant. What's important is the overall context and its demonstration of the value of persistence.

It's harder to believe that even superstar Michael Jordan was cut from his high school basketball team, but this only served to make him more determined to persist—and consistently succeed as the league's most valuable player. It's not only how good you are, but also how badly you want it. Winners do what losers didn't.

How often do you hear about people with great ideas or talent who never follow through? They're jealous of those who have become what they see as an 'overnight success' without recognising the amount of work invested in laying the groundwork for that success.

A woman recently asked me for advice on becoming a professional speaker and exclaimed: 'I'm willing to give everything it takes and dedicate six weeks to becoming a full-time speaker.'

She was deflated when I informed her that I'd spent years speaking for free before earning a fee. This 'wanna be' speaker had mistakenly thought it was an easy way to earn a living. Another, commenting on the success of my book, added:

'I could have written a book like *The Power of One*, but . . .' Her chain of excuses was endless, with a refusal to recognise that best-selling Australian author Bryce Courtenay expended countless hours of blood, sweat and tears finishing that book. The key word is *finish*. Millions of people start books, but in spite of holding down a responsible job, dealing with family crises, plus coping with the mundane duties of daily living that could easily have diverted lesser writers, Courtenay actually completed *The Power of One:* a brilliant novel about following dreams. Critics never talk about the lonely hours writing in the middle of the night when friends are partying or nestled snugly in bed, or the frustration of revisions. Still, Courtenay, like authors before him, persisted in his passion for the pen. Like most first-time writers, he faced rejection by publishers, just as we all face rejection in some form. Yet, in spite of the obstacles, he pursued his path to become one of Australia's best-selling authors. He'll go down in history as an author—not a 'would be' or a 'could be' but a genuine author. Just as Edison wasn't a tinkerer but a true scientist and Jordan didn't just dribble but delivered. All were champions because they persisted. Whether in the realm of science, literature, sport, business or any endeavour, never forget the PQ. As Mum always said: 'Mind your Ps and Qs'.

It will help, as you traverse the ups and downs of life's journey, to know that:

'If you travel a path with no obstacles, it probably doesn't lead anywhere.'

20

'The only one thing of which I am certain is that there is very little about which one can be certain.'

W. Somerset Maugham

'I don't know'. 'I'm not sure.' 'Who knows?' These are phrases you would seldom have heard a manager utter in past decades. After all, the boss was supposed to have all the answers. Isn't that what justified his (and it usually was a male) higher salary, the corner office and a company car? Many had reached their so-called leadership roles by diligently working their way up the corporate ladder in the one organisation, learning the business from the grass roots in the days when it was expected that they and the company were unlikely to ever part. If they did a reasonable job, they had a reasonable job—for life. With that came the luxury of nurturing a field of specific knowledge to help the simultaneous security of the individual and the business.

The manager might well have been able to give an immediate answer to a specific problem on the factory floor because he'd worked there himself at one time and could delve into the toolkit of his past experience. That reservoir is no longer so replete, given the ever-increasing complexity of the workplace. Most general managers wouldn't have a clue about marketing on the Internet, how to write a robotics program or the latest industrial relations ruling from the government. And guess what? That's OK.

Because what a good manager now needs is an inquiring mind and the ability to surround himself or herself with the people who do know the answers—or are at least in a position to find someone who does. A good manager needs to ask the right questions. They lose credibility and customers if they only pretend to have the answers and don't.

Leaders gain respect and loyalty if they can create a climate which encourages each and every employee to be empowered and come up with unique solutions to constantly changing situations in the marketplace; to recognise that uncertainty is a way of life. Those who can best accept this ambiguity can best manage it to their advantage.

So relax. It's OK not to have all the answers as long as you never stop asking the questions— questions about how you and your organisation can not only survive, but continually improve in a rapidly changing and increasingly uncertain world.

Whoever said that death and taxes were the only certainties may still be right—unless, of course, you believe that the soul never dies and tax avoidance is possible with a good accountant and a bank account in the Bahamas.

We all live with varying degrees of uncertainty whether we like it or not, so we may as well accept it as a fact of life. We love pleasant surprises, and a totally predictable life—to my way of thinking— would be somewhat dull. It's those unpleasant surprises which we find harder to deal with—a traffic detour when we're running late, a retrenchment when we can least afford the loss of income, an illness when we're too busy to be sick. None of these things is ever planned and they can range from mildly annoying to totally debilitating. So maybe it's better if we don't bank on absolutes quite so much and more willingly accept that uncertainty is a way of life which can't be altered by being more upset about it.

Admittedly, accepting uncertainty is far easier to write about than actually do! I still prefer to explain things by logic or by precedent but increasingly realise that there are many unexplainable phenomena that don't readily lend themselves to such explanation. When I was seventeen, I 'knew' certain things were so. I now recognise—albeit reluctantly at times—that this is no longer the case. The more I know, the more I realise how much I don't know!

Maybe that means I've learned something along the way because, whether it be in our professional or personal lives, in this age of uncertainty nearly a century and a half after Somerset Maugham was

born, his words are even more poignant than ever
in that:

*'The only one thing of which I am certain is that
there is very little about which one can be certain.'*

21

'The most important things in life aren't things.'

Anon

I'd like to say that I'm not a materialistic person. That's what I'd like to say—but it wouldn't be true! I enjoy living in a lovely home with all the modern conveniences and driving a nice car. I know I have more clothes than I need in my closet, more paintings on the wall than necessary, more CDs than I can play at a time and more crockery than I'll ever use, even when entertaining. Occasionally I feel guilty, knowing that others in the world have no material possessions whatsoever—especially when I think that many of my things have been bought while travelling to third-world countries where even my camera would be worth more money than an average yearly income!

A few of these possessions are expensive, but most are purely sentimental. Like most people, if the house were to burn down, I'd leave all the expensive things behind and try to save the photographs—worthless bits of images on paper to anyone else, but priceless memories that I could never replace.

Having been burgled, I know that my insurance policy covers replacement of most items. On the last occasion, friends were astounded at how relatively calm I was about the stolen goods: 'Well, at least they didn't take the photos and no one hit me over the head.' Admittedly, I was less than thrilled about the invasion of privacy, loss of sentimental jewellery that was a family heirloom and the hassle of filling in forms and replacing the stolen goods. I also knew that in a few years' time, I'd never miss what was taken and know that there's more to life than mere money.

There are too many more important things that we can never replace—the love of a parent or child, our health or the time lost by wasting a day. Some-one asked what I wanted Santa to bring for Christmas last year. As I was frantically trying to get cards mailed, presents bought and still run a business, all I really wanted was a big bucket of time! Like health and love, it's one of the most important things in my life and can never be replaced.

A longtime role model and one of the best managers I've ever had always made time to listen to his staff, even when he probably didn't have time to do so. As a manager myself, I was often guilty of not following Bert Keddie's lead as I was often busy focusing on processes that I thought would make the organisation a success.

A multi-millionaire friend of mine says that success is being able to do what he wants, when he wants, how he wants and with whom he wants. A self-made man, he hasn't always been wealthy but now no longer needs to earn a cent to support himself in his expensive lifestyle for the rest of his life. What then drives him to continually take on new challenges? Is it accumulating wealth for the sake of wealth? Ego? Insecurity? The thrill of the challenge? To leave a legacy or large inheritance to his children? To avoid boredom? To be better than the Joneses? Or simply because he wants to?

I suspect it's the last-mentioned and hasten to add that, although he has every material possession known to mankind, he is also one of the most generous men I know. He is the first to assist a charity or a friend in need. He's generous with both his wealth and his wealth of knowledge in giving his time to help others achieve their own dreams. He readily admits that he wasn't always that way and for many years, when he was struggling, felt he had to always beat the other guy in a dog eat dog world. But now he believes that the more you give, the more you get in return.

Even though he can have any material possession he wishes, he's not at all like the apocryphal story of the young yuppie who was involved in a car accident. As the young man gains consciousness and looks at the wreckage of his expensive car, he wails:

'Oh no, my Porsche, my Porsche.'

The ambulance officers try unsuccessfully to pacify him, but still he cries:

'Oh no, my Porsche, my Porsche.'

Finally an ambulance officer grabs him in exasperation and points out that his left arm is severed from the elbow down, to which the young man now cries:

'Oh no, my Rolex, my Rolex.'

Maybe, at one time or another, we've all been a bit like the young yuppie—guilty of forgetting what is truly important in our lives, forgetting that material possessions aren't as important as our health and relationships, forgetting that life isn't about having things but about doing things, forgetting that . . .

'The most important things in life aren't things.'

22

'Rather than close a sale, open a relationship.'

Denis Waitley

Salespeople have traditionally been trained to close a sale and obtain their commission without much consideration about how to retain the customer. In today's marketing environment, the importance of building long-term customer relationships cannot be over-emphasised. It's imperative to take into consideration not only the lifetime value of each individual transaction, but the opportunity to cross-sell to that satisfied customer, and also to calculate the number of other people that they are likely to refer to your organisation.

According to a global survey by Touche Consulting (*Sydney Morning Herald*, 17/11/98), 85 per cent of financial institutions believe that retaining customers is the major challenge in the future, yet only one in five is, in fact, securing long-term relationships with its customers.

A slight variation in interest rates usually isn't enough to entice people to switch banks, given the detailed legal requirements to open a new account. Most banks don't win customers through advertising campaigns; rather, they lose them through poor service, when the frustration level reaches such a peak that a customer is willing to go through the hassle of changing.

That's why it's crucial that every employee realises the important role they play in retaining loyal customers by looking at ways to say 'yes' to requests, rather than resorting to the rule book to look for justifications to say 'no'. I'm not suggesting that banks—or any other organisation—act unethically or take on unprofitable customers, but rather that they look at altering their approach that the customer is always wrong.

A number of years ago, I had funds in term deposits of two different financial institutions, and required the cash unexpectedly. When I phoned the first to withdraw the money, the employee curtly said:

'Don't you know it's a term deposit and can't be withdrawn before the due date, dummy?' In fairness, she didn't actually say 'dummy' but her tone of voice certainly implied that!

In contrast, the second bank responded:

'Of course we can make the money available immediately. You do realise though that because it is a term deposit, you will lose interest.'

When I checked with the first bank, they in

fact had the same policy, but one employee was coming from a position of 'no' while the other was coming from a position of 'yes'. When it came time to reinvest the money, it doesn't take much thought to realise I put it all in the second bank because I perceived they placed more value on customer relationships than on rule books. They had earned my repeat business through their attitude.

Customer loyalty can't be bought. It must be earned and, like the loyalty of long-term friends, it accumulates like compound interest—genuine interest in the needs and wants of the customer. Many organisations spend millions of dollars creating loyalty reward programs. These have many advantages but are still not as powerful as the more lasting loyalty programs that start and finish with outstanding personalised customer service that makes the customer feel truly appreciated and not taken for granted.

Nor can staff be taken for granted if you want to maintain customer loyalty.

I frequently stop for freshly squeezed juice after my run along the beach and one morning noticed a young waiter who I'd assumed was the owner of another cappuccino cafe down the road.

'Did you sell your business?' I asked.

'Oh no, I wish it was mine. I left because they didn't appreciate me. You know how it is,' he replied with a shrug and half-smile of resignation.

I was surprised as he had always seemed so helpful and appeared to treat the cafe and customers as if it were indeed his own business. What a valuable asset the employer lost by ignoring the need for appreciation to be shown in staff relationships. And, yes, I did know 'how it was', as that was one of the contributing factors that prompted me to leave the corporate world.

Neither this local cafe or juice bar had any formal loyalty programs in place but as I observed, I noticed the young waiter cheerily chatting to other customers who he had obviously established a relationship with at the other cafe. Loyalty to staff contributes to loyal customers.

I'm a member of about half a dozen airline frequent flier programs and countless hotel so-called loyalty programs. I happily accumulate points and whatever benefits are associated with those points. Without question, there are times when the availability of such points does indeed influence my purchasing decision and—especially if all other things are equal—like most people, I opt for the points.

However, all things are seldom equal in terms of the past service I've received! And sometimes loyalty programs aren't worth the plastic card that they're written on! I once had my wallet stolen, containing all my credit cards and identification. Arriving at my destination after a long flight to pick up a rental car, I only then realised to my horror that I didn't have my driver's licence. Nor did I have my rental car loyalty card but the latter wasn't a problem as the company had all my details on computer, including my licence number. However, their policy was firmly: 'No licence, no car', which I must admit was a fair thing.

As I walked despondently away from the busy counter, which had a partnership agreement with the airline on which I'd just arrived, I noticed that a competitor's rental desk didn't have a single customer in the queue. Thinking I had nothing to lose, I explained my situation to the young man at the desk and was able to give him the exact date of when one of my clients had last hired a car on my behalf. Much to my surprise, he candidly admitted that their computer records didn't go back that far. He then astounded me by saying: 'You look like an honest woman and I can't imagine anyone would have made up that date because you wouldn't have known our records couldn't prove otherwise. So I'm happy to hire you a car as long as you sign a waiver that your licence has been stolen.'

I was so impressed that I gave him an autographed copy of my best-selling book on customer service. And, even though I don't have a loyalty card with that company, guess what my rental car company of choice will be in future!

Here was an example of where all other things weren't equal.

There are many other instances when I prefer to visit a hotel (or shop or restaurant or whatever) that doesn't have a formal loyalty program in place. They don't buy my loyalty but earn it through their consistent care—through remembering my name; through making me feel special; through realising that they're not in the hotel, airline or restaurant business but the people business; through remembering that they should:

'Rather than close a sale, open a relationship.'

23

'Work is a journey, not a destination.'

Catherine DeVrye

This is more than a cliché for the high percentage of today's busy managers, for whom business travel has become a way of life. While some still relish the thrill of travel, for the frequent flier that joy has worn as thin as the tattered leather on the briefcase they carry. Each hotel room starts to look the same and often they see no more of a city than the passing landscape in the taxi between the airport and the office.

Most seasoned travellers complain of the long hours spent on planes or taxis, waiting in lounges, away from family or friends. While concentrating on the key reason for the business trip, your mind can't help but wander and worry about the other projects you're also juggling back at the office. You're conscious of the need to recharge your mobile phone, when you really wish it was as easy to recharge your own batteries by plugging yourself into a human-sized wall socket, before complete loss of energy at the most inconvenient moment! Yet, in spite of modems—or maybe because of them—that difficult-to-define feeling of being disconnected remains.

When did you start travelling? Was it your exit from the womb? When you first left hospital in your mother's arms to go to a place called home? Or was it when you crawled or took those first tentative steps on your own that you began travelling: your own journey of self.

Although I fly 500 000 kilometres a year, I know that actual physical travel is only part of the bigger journey. I travelled to primary school on my bicycle, high school on a bus and by the time I reached university, I had the exquisite freedom of my own car. We all probably remember our first trip away from home on our own, whether it was to a school camp, to stay with friends or relatives or to attend a sporting event. Travel is a natural state for humans.

Even those who can only envy others who fly to exotic destinations are still travellers. As long as health permits, there's barely a day we don't journey from our home, even if only to stand in a queue at the supermarket.

While all this physical travel is happening, another emotional journey is simultaneously in progress. Our minds wander far and wide, covering more territory than our bodies possibly could, even in ten lifetimes. Sometimes we control our direction, while at other times we find ourselves thinking unexplained thoughts. If we were embarking on a physical trip, we'd have a plan, probably in the form of a map or itinerary. But we seldom do so with our own inner journeys. We seldom take time out of our frantic schedules to plan where that journey may lead. We're too busy being busy and rushing for the next flight.

At 30 000 feet in the air, it's no wonder we seldom feel grounded in the present moment, unaware of what is truly important in our lives. Rush, rush, rush! And, with that rushing, we sometimes feel that we are only moving in circles in a holding pattern and questioning if we're really as important as we thought we were. Yet each person reading this book is important. We can and do make a difference. First, however, we have to prioritise what really is or isn't important in the bigger picture of our busy lives. Movement without purpose is like a bicycle without wheels.

Travel is exciting—you can see new places and meet new people—but I urge you to take some time to travel within because we all, whether we're willing to admit it or not, actually need some time to be alone within ourselves and our own private thoughts.

Here are a few travel tips for inner journeys on a business trip:

Plan to arrive 30 minutes earlier than recommended for a flight, so as not to be rushed. Treat yourself to a leisurely cup of coffee or, better still, herbal tea or fresh fruit juice, just to unwind.

You can politely choose not to speak to the person sitting next to you or you may be surprised to learn something from them. Always have a book, memo or other convenient 'prop' with which to excuse yourself, in case they are boring you with their life story, problems at work or string of accomplishments, but be open to the prospect that it may be a fortuitous meeting.

Flying is an ideal time to practise meditation or deep breathing; an oasis in the sky to relax without the phone constantly ringing (let's hope mobiles are never allowed on flights!)

Don't wait for your boss or shareholders to give you your annual appraisal. DIY and praise yourself. Remember the praise in ap*prais*al. We're often too hard on ourselves, and beating ourselves up only bruises the ego. A healthy ego, versus an egotistical one, is a good thing.

Ask yourself if this is where you'd be by choice and, if not, why not and what do you plan to do about it? By when?

Rather than worry about all the last-minute things that you didn't finish at the office, take a moment to congratulate yourself on all the things that you *did* manage to achieve this day, week or month.

Yes, the glamour may have worn off your business trips long ago. For many of us, boarding a jet is little different to boarding a bus to go to work.

Dr Robert Schuller said 'Success is a journey, not a destination' but I have modified this to remind you to take care and take the time to remember that:

'Work is a journey, not a destination.'

24

'When you're green, you're growing. When you're ripe, you rot.'

Ray Kroc, founder of McDonald's

From the time of conception, we start our never-ending journey of growth. From womb to tomb, it is a path paved with a mottled mixture of joy and frustration.

From the moment we come kicking and screaming into this world, we increasingly take more responsibility for our own growth and development. We quickly learn the source of food and nurturing, and that our expressive cries will help communicate our increasingly complex needs.

From crawling to our first tentative steps, we are encouraged to make more and more progress. In early days, proud parents gleefully plot our growth, measuring our weight at birth until we stand taller and taller against a colourful chart on the wall.

'I can't believe how much you've grown,' comment well-meaning adults—a phrase that begins to annoy us as we do indeed grow into adolescence.

From the first day of school, someone else appears to take responsibility for our intellectual growth and development. Teachers water and nurture us in an educational jungle, but are never ultimately responsible for our growth. We can't yet see the forest for the trees and don't realise that it is only us who have that responsibility. Some flourish more readily than others in this formal educational environment and growth is measured by progress from one grade to the next.

Reaching adolescence, we become conspicuously conscious about our physical growth, constantly comparing ourselves to others in the mirror or locker room. Changes in hormones throughout puberty easily define our growth and we can't wait to 'grow up'—as if that will magically solve all our adolescent traumas and replace doubts with the certainty which grown-ups appear to have on the surface. Little do we know!

Physical growth peaks before we turn 21. We've moved on to university or the workforce but no longer does anyone comment on our growth. When was the last time someone said: 'My, how you've grown' . . . and just as well! In a perfect world, we'd feel as good at 80 as we did at 18 and be as smart at 80 as we thought we were at 18!

Maybe you no longer have hair growing on your head while it sprouts from your nostrils. Your waist grows outward, there are ulcers in your stomach, cataracts on your eyes or, worse still, the dreaded growth of white cells feared to be cancer. But, what of cancer of the mind? Growth for growth's sake is not necessarily a good thing in individuals or organisations. Nor is stagnation.

Employees and employers alike look for more in terms of personal growth than the simple escalation of the bottom line: how to strike a balance between profits and the perils of growth, in our ever-changing environment.

Many have found lifelong partners to grow with them on their journey and are frantically juggling work and home life. Too often, the once-ideal marriage of two well-intentioned individuals is no longer a marriage of minds, values and common goals, as time sees them grow apart. There is an initial sense of failure and then, hopefully, new growth for both.

Often, through such painful processes as divorce, death and illness, we actually grow stronger. Like trees, when pruned, we boost our individual strength to stand against the winds of change, stronger than before. We grow if we sow seeds of hope.

We come to realise, however traumatically, that no one is ultimately responsible for our growth but ourselves. Still, we ponder how we can best grow. By sitting mindlessly in front of the television or watching an educational video? By leaning on a smelly bar stool or drinking up the beauty of a clear mountain stream? By loving the sound of our own voice or listening to others who share a different perspective? By constantly looking outward or taking some of that precious time—by far our most valuable natural resource—to look inward to better understand what else we require for our growth in the next stage of our ever-embryonic development.

We grow inward by looking outward. And we grow outward by looking inward. Emotional and spiritual growth blossoms. What sort of mental and emotional nutrients are you exposed to? Or are you poisoning your path of continuous growth with noxious weeds wasting your all too precious time on the planet?

If you think you know it all, you're ripe and rotting—an endangered species as younger people surpass you for promotion at work, while you close your eyes to advances in technology in a truly global market. It is predicted that people will have at least five career changes in their lives, no longer the steady job of yesteryear.

Yet some people have already succumbed to hardening of the intellectual arteries when they're still in their twenties, while others remain immune to such degeneration well past their nineties. What's the difference? The differentiating factor is that the latter group never feels that they know it all. They never lose sight of their roots firmly anchored to a bed of continuous learning and improvement. They know they need a thirst for knowledge as surely as a plant needs water to grow.

They realise that they may be transplanted to a greener pasture, need to prune some unnecessary tasks or need supplements for further growth and development. They read books, listen to tapes, attend conferences or take every opportunity to simply speak to others from wide-ranging fields of expertise—people outside their own particular field of knowledge.

Along their journey, they have filtered the steady stream of new information available and decided which is right for them. Their growth is truly consolidated when they act on their chosen path. Too many people think they're growing by only absorbing what others say and never actually taking the necessary steps to transform theory into action themselves.

Meanwhile, others are simultaneously taking action and opening their eyes to the wonders of the universe. They're taking time from the hustle and bustle to see the serenity of a sunset, hear a babbling brook, inhale the intoxicating perfume of a flower, taste pure rainwater or reach out to touch a stranger in need. These gifts have been here all along but we were often too busy 'growing up' to appreciate the childlike wonders of the world.

As life goes full circle—from womb to tomb—the happiest people in the world are still growing, with minds more fertile than ever as they draw their last breath, knowing that we humans have more than one dimension and that:

'When you're green, you're growing. When you're ripe, you rot.'

25

'There is no comparison between what we lose by not succeeding and what we lose by not trying.'

Catherine DeVrye

People often ask how I became a professional speaker. I'd like to say that it happened overnight, but there were many circumstances conspiring to point me in that direction and more hurdles than I ever would have imagined along the way. Certainly it wasn't a career I'd considered as a child and I had been in the workplace over twenty years before even contemplating the possibilities of earning a living by opening my mouth. After all, I was raised to believe that little girls should be seen and not heard; even decades later, the prospect of speaking to total strangers was inconceivable.

While in a senior management role at IBM, I found myself signing cheques for the trainers and motivational speakers we used for our management programs and sales incentive events. Some represented money well spent and others were a dubious investment, to say the least.

Prior to a major conference, one well-known speaker cancelled at the last moment because of a family emergency and it seemed impossible to obtain someone of similar credentials in a short space of time. As it was a topic with which I was familiar, I volunteered to fill the void. Rather than be pleased that I had offered to do something well outside my job description, my boss chastened: 'Don't be ridiculous. We need an expert.'

In spite of assuring him that my first university degree was in that subject area, he insisted I find an 'expert'. A couple of days later, I informed him that we'd located a visiting professor from Harvard University who was on sabbatical in Australia. Much to my relief, he asked no questions. There was no such person and I had decided to don a short curly blonde wig and glasses to pose as the expert. (I'm brunette!)

It initially seemed a good idea, but I was more than a little nervous when I finally stepped on stage in front of 200 colleagues and customers. After the first few minutes, I enjoyed every second and was relieved to receive laughter and applause. The executive, who had initially hired me years earlier, took notes in the front row and didn't even recognise me! As the Master of Ceremonies thanked me for sharing my wealth of knowledge to shed new light on a familiar topic, I removed the wig and glasses and said:

'It's me. Often, we know this stuff ourselves but feel we need an outside expert to validate our beliefs.'

As shock and laughter subsided, and the audience appeared happy knowing that I did, in fact, have subject matter expertise, it became obvious just how difficult it is to 'be a prophet in your own land'.

Only my immediate boss was furious.

'That was risky. What if it had failed?'

'But it didn't,' I protested.

His paternalistic approach reminded me of my mother. 'Be careful, dear,' she'd always say. Our parents seldom encouraged us to take risks and I know I certainly never heard:

'Go out and play and take lots of risks, dear.'

From an early age, we're conditioned to play it safe and this is certainly so in a conservative corporation. Yet playing safe is sometimes the riskiest thing we can do. As John F. Kennedy once said:

'There are risks and costs to a program of action. But they are far less than the long-range costs and risks of comfortable inaction.'

My boss seemed unimpressed when I quoted Kennedy. I knew it was indeed risky to pull such a spoof but I knew it was more risky to have someone else with questionable credentials or a gap in the conference program. Soon I was speaking to IBM managers throughout Australia and New Zealand at our annual management forums—but never again with a wig and glasses!

Through word-of-mouth demand, IBM started charging me out to their clients on a fee-for-service basis and I began to think that if they'd pay IBM, maybe they'd pay me directly. That's when I decided to take another risk and become a professional speaker.

I realised that there was a growing market for high-content speakers (versus snake oil salesmen and women) who, through careful briefing, could repackage a management message for executives who were looking for different ways to present their own messages in a motivational way.

Five years later, IBM was now one of my clients and I was speaking at their sales incentive event in Korea.

'When I used to work for IBM, management would have paid me to be quiet. Now, they're paying me to speak—what a marvelous transition!' My former boss's boss was in the audience and he laughed as loudly as everyone else did, knowing that it is indeed difficult to be a prophet in one's own land.

That's when I realised that, rather than have a passive career in an organisation, I could have a passionate one—in or out of the organisation—and that passion could indeed become my profession.

We can all do likewise if we're willing to take calculated, not foolhardy, risks and step outside our comfort zone with greater confidence. I recently asked a now semi-retired, Harvard educated doyen of Australian industry what he might do differently in his career. I was surprised when he confided that he wished he'd been more confident earlier on. It's hard to imagine that this outstanding leader, chairman of countless boards and role model and friend to me as well as to countless others, could have achieved much more than he had in his career. He may have wished he'd had more confidence in the early days but, unlike some, he'd never need to worry about the remorse others may feel lying on their deathbeds and knowing that they were 'past it', when they were never really there in terms of realising their true potential.

There's no better moment than this one to put plans in place to do what you truly want to do. Some ventures will admittedly be riskier than others. Some will be more successful and some may fail completely but . . . to lose is not to fail. The only failure is to lose and not try again because . . .

'There is no comparison between what we lose by not succeeding and what we lose by not trying.'

26

**'It can take years to win a customer
and only seconds to lose one.'**

Catherine DeVrye

We work our butts off to gain repeat business because we know it costs five times more to obtain a new customer than to retain an existing one. We've learned about the loyalty ladder of turning suspects to prospects to customers to clients to advocates. We know the value of word-of-mouth advertising. We've read that a 5 per cent increase in customer loyalty can mean up to an 85 per cent increase in profits. Many organisations have even invested millions of dollars developing loyalty incentive programs.

But just how loyal are customers? And staff? Is there any correlation between the two and what can management do to increase loyalty? With takeovers and retrenchments, many employees are sceptical about loyalty because they don't feel they receive any from their employer. Loyalty is never a one-way street.

Customers are also cynical when they see expensive advertising campaigns with enticing offers to attract new customers, but feel that they—the existing customers—are often ignored and taken for granted by the supplier.

Sales training has historically focused on closing a sale. Too often, sales representatives have been successful in getting the order but then forgetting the customer, possibly because their commission programs didn't take retention into account.

Customer and staff loyalty must be earned like the loyalty of long-term friends or pets. A friend has a sign on her fridge:

'The more I know men, the more I love my dog.'

She laments that she has been unable to find a man as loyal and loving as her faithful pooch and I'm sure any canine-loving males reading this could say the same about females, as a man's best friend is always glad to see them and never nags!

What's more, dogs endear themselves to us by wagging their tails instead of their tongues; something worth remembering in the workplace as well! Although I deplore gossip, I must confess to times in the past when I've succumbed to it. When I left IBM, another female colleague who departed at the same time took the initiative to set up a network of IBM women. It was a marvellous idea and we would often comment that it was a pity that we hadn't been more supportive of each other within the corporation, rather than sometimes feeling another might be a threat and thus lose a potential opportunity through petty jealousy or turf guarding—both of which are best left for the dogs.

When my golden retriever had ten pups, I offered to donate one of Tam's litter to the Guide Dog Association. In doing so, I learned a valuable management lesson when the trainer informed me that there are two sorts of dogs that flunk out of guide dog school.

One is the dog that is totally disobedient. It tears up your possessions, growls and refuses to stay still on the lead. You'd expect that sort of dog to fail. But, strange as it sounds, the other sort of dog which fails is the one that is totally obedient. As I looked puzzled, the trainer explained:

'Picture yourself at a major intersection. You're blind and have your dog. You command the dog: "Go!" Without questioning whether or not to obey you, it goes!'

The trainer went on to explain that the dogs which passed were the ones labelled 'selectively disobedient,' with emphasis on the word 'selectively'. They would assess the situation and then block your path to save you from a semi-trailer which might have killed you if the dog had blindly obeyed the command.

In most modern organisations, employees are, in many ways, like good guide dogs. They don't simply obey without thinking of the consequences. They no longer assume that the boss is always right and has all the answers.

The ideal employee is one who assesses every situation and may often be 'selectively disobedient' for the good of everyone. The key is to create a spirit of trust within an organisation so that no one—no matter how junior or lowly they may be in the pecking order—is frightened to turn to the boss and say:

'Hey, I think there's a better way.'

This sort of corporate culture would literally save management from the equivalent of a semi-trailer, in the form of the competition which could be about to flatten your organisation. To be more profitable, employers must allow employees to be more profit-able by ensuring that unnecessary barriers to bureaucracy are removed.

In a day and age where many employees expect more from work than just a pay cheque, it is crucial to create an environment which instils long-term loyalty and trust and treats both employees and customers as you would like to be treated. After all, if you don't look after your staff, they won't look after your customers. And you have no hope of making your numbers if you treat employees like numbers.

Although people aren't dogs, there are lessons management could learn from them about creating loyalty and trust in employees. Like finding new customers, it takes a lot longer to go through the process of hiring competent new staff than it does to look after your existing ones. It's far better to focus on rewarding desired behaviour, as illustrated by another dog story:

A blind man and his dog weave in and out of the traffic across a major street. After they miraculously reach the other side in one piece, the blind man reaches in his pocket to give the dog a biscuit. A passer-by, who witnessed the dangerous crossing, says: 'If I were you I wouldn't reward that dog—it almost got you killed.'

The blind man responds:

'I'm not rewarding it, I'm just finding where its mouth is so I can kick it in the butt!'

To create staff loyalty, it's important to tell staff how well they are doing and not just give them a boot in the butt when things go wrong.

It's also important to let your regular customers know—often—how much you appreciate their business rather than wait until they've left or are about to do so. It's too late then to try and win back their loyalty because like friends:

'It can take years to win a customer and only seconds to lose one.'

27

'Businesses don't fail. People fail.'

Paul Simons quoting Bill Wylie

How often do you hear managers espouse that people are an organisation's most valuable asset while readily pointing the finger of blame at those same people if something goes wrong. It's much easier to say: 'My secretary forgot'; 'the production foreman overlooked it'; or 'the supplier is always late' than to admit a mistake yourself.

It takes great courage and integrity to accept responsibility at the top for any failure and to take action to correct it for the future.

Admittedly, people do fail and they do make mistakes. But it is a greater failing if those mistakes are repeated, if the employee is reprimanded without any corresponding learning taking place, or if a manager can't say sorry.

It's too easy to overlook the fact that quality products and quality services all begin and end with quality people. It's also seldom appreciated just how many people might contribute to the end product that arrives in the hands of a happy customer.

I often speak to organisations which most of us have never heard of because they're not household brand names. I've been awed by the magnitude of interdependence and this became blatantly obvious at a recent conference in a cotton-growing region of northern New South Wales. As a consumer who buys cotton clothing or sheets, I hadn't fully appreciated the complexity of this business-to-business relationship, simply because–like most customers– I'd never stopped to think about it.

A representative from a multinational chemical company preceded me on stage and spoke to an agricultural sales group about the wide array of insecticide sprays and fertilisers that they could recommend to farmers. The farmers, in turn, supply the cotton to a cooperative; it then goes to a weaving mill, to a designer, to a production line at a factory, to a finished garment, to a wholesaler, to a distributor–all this until I finally might buy a shirt from a retail outlet.

Of course, I've omitted the many other organisations that contribute to the supply of raw materials to manufacture the chemical in the first place, the machinery required to do so and other such processes as packaging, printing of labels, ink supply for those labels and professional services. The list is endless and so therefore are the opportunities for something to go wrong along the way to the end-user customer.

This multi-faceted process, which happens in virtually any industry, can be likened to a domino effect: if one domino falls over, the others do likewise. The same is true of a relay race. If one person drops the baton the team fails; the race is won by the team that can do faster and smoother transfers. The same is true in business.

Whether speaking of internal or external customers, think of a customer as the baton in a relay. If you were a member of an Olympic relay team, you would have two responsibilities. One would be to add value with every step you take while you're personally carrying the baton, the customer. However, as a member of a relay team, you have another responsibility: to understand the strengths, weaknesses and speed of whoever is passing you the baton and practise that smooth transfer—then to do likewise with whoever you're passing the baton on to.

There's an old saying that any team is only as strong as its weakest link. This applies whether there are four people on an Olympic relay team or 40, 400 or 4000 people on an organisational team. There can be record-breaking performances in one section, but if someone in another department drops the baton along the way, the race for customer loyalty could well and truly be lost. Sure, it takes time to practise the smooth transfer from one area to another, but it takes a lot longer to have to stop and pick up the baton—or the pieces.

124

Customers don't really care who dropped the baton along the way. They're only interested in the final delivery across the finishing line. Like me, most consumers take the steps required to deliver the final product for granted. I was admittedly now more aware of what it takes to produce a cotton garment, but would that mean I'd be any more understanding if I wanted to buy a new set of sheets and they were out of stock? Would I care that it may have been the fault of one individual or one team, somewhere along the line, who failed to deliver what they said they would? Would I be happy to listen to excuses from the person I was dealing with?

Probably not! I'd likely just go to another shop. Furthermore, if I was one of many customers who had similar experiences, that shop probably wouldn't be in business for long, simply because:

'Businesses don't fail. People fail.'

28

'Health is wealth—and tax free!'

Anon

We can place tangible dollar values on our car, house, TV set, dishwasher, kettle, etc. In fact, we could roughly add up the sum total of all of our many assets to get a pretty accurate estimate of our 'wealth'. Most of us have those goods insured for replacement value. Yet we seldom think to place a value on our greatest asset—our own health, which can never be replaced. It's something that we usually take for granted until, for some reason, we no longer have it. Only then do we fully realise that without good health it's almost impossible to fully enjoy anything else, including the other valuable assets of friends and family.

We're often so busy accumulating physical goods that we feel we're too busy to look after our own physical well-being. People often ask how I find time in my busy travel schedule to fit in exercise. I admit that it's not always easy but I know, and remind them, that if we're too busy to look after our own health, we're too busy. Full stop! And, if you don't take care of your physical body, where else do you plan to live?

They ask how I can afford the time to exercise daily. I reply that I can't afford *not* to take the time. Admittedly, it's sometimes difficult to get up on a cold winter morning and getting started is usually the hardest part. But I also know that I feel so rejuvenated after exercise that I often wonder why it was such a struggle to get going in the first place.

I often hear comments that you're going to die anyway from something or other so why worry about staying fit. I agree that, indeed, all of our bodies will indeed stop functioning and if we have the misfortune of being hit by the proverbial bus tomorrow, it wouldn't matter whether we were or were not in reasonable physical shape. By the same token, it's also true that there are certain preventative measures we *can* take to increase not just the quantity of our life, but the quality along the way. We can all enjoy a feeling of wellness and vitality that comes with regular exercise, a healthier diet and some quiet time to recharge our own batteries.

Entire books have been written on various methods of achieving optimal results in these areas. Most contain sound advice, even when advocating some fad diet, exercise regime or relaxation technique. I've read many, readily embraced some ideas for a time, dropped some and completely rejected others. So what really does work? It has to be something that you feel will work for *you*! It needs to become not just a one-week wonder, but a way of life that you believe you will be able to stick to—one that isn't so arduous that it will be easy to give up. Whether you join a gym, exercise with friends, get a personal trainer or do it yourself, each individual needs to find their own level of what they believe is achievable. Without question, the key ingredient for any program, regardless of what the program is, is to do it regularly and build it into your daily routine, as surely as brushing your teeth.

I've often struggled with weight and love chocolate. In fact, in my ideal world, chocolate would be a vegetable! During my twenties and thirties, my weight crept up little by little. Although I wasn't obese, I was two sizes larger than when I left university. Looking down at my bikini one day, I was appalled at the little roll of fat. 'Where did it come from?' I thought.

But I knew! And I had known for a number of years but just let it happen. I then decided to lose 10 kilos, which sounded rather daunting until I wrote down a plan for doing so over a six-month period and realised that, according to my plan, I'd only need to lose a little every day, which didn't seem nearly so daunting.

I'd read that supermodel Elle McPherson did 500 sit-ups per day. Well, I'd be happy if I looked a tenth as good as her, so decided to build up to 50, starting with five. It was hard at first and my little inner voice could always come up with excuses as to why I couldn't exercise or why I needed more chocolate but I stuck to my plan and eventually it became a routine and not at all arduous.

I've read that if you do something continually for 21 days, it becomes a habit. I have a feeling that it took me a lot longer but I did not even begin to imagine the difference it made to my general well-being. Sure, I've still had bouts of bronchitis along the way but have recovered more quickly than before. Regular exercise not only adds years to your life, but life to those years.

A few simple hints, regardless of whether you want to walk up a flight of stairs without puffing or are training for a marathon, are:

- Write down your *personal* realistic goal—for example, to lose 5 kilos or to run 5 kilometres.

- Write down your *personal* action plan with progressive steps for improvement. For example:
    - to walk for _____ minutes every day for two weeks. After two weeks, increase distance or time to _____.
    - to have ____ alcohol free days per week or ____ sugar free days; or have caffeine only ____ per day.

- Monitor your progress with a chart on your fridge door or bathroom mirror. You won't see improvement every day but it's a good incentive to look at the trends.

- Reward yourself for attaining each goal along the way. However, if, for example, you're focusing on weight loss, don't reward yourself with a big binge meal. Rather, treat yourself to your favourite perfume, tickets to a concert or something else you'd enjoy that won't undo all your good work. Of course, the biggest intangible reward will be your overall well-being.

Didn't someone once say that despite the increase in the cost of living, the demand for it increases. Isn't that the truth! That's why it's imperative to remember that:

'Health is wealth—and tax free!'

29

'You can't discover new oceans until you have the courage to lose sight of the shore.'

André Gide

Whether surfing the breakers or surfing the Net, it requires steely nerve to be in a position to smoothly ride out the ever-constant waves of change on land or sea.

It takes the courage of your convictions to change long-established patterns of behaviour—actions that have come to seem as timeless as the sea itself. You know the ones . . . all part of the 'we've always done it that way' syndrome with which we're so familiar at work.

The surf culture seems the antithesis to the business one. Yet, surprisingly, there are lessons to be learned for those of us who spend considerably more time in blue suits than in wetsuits! In fact, we can learn from each other.

As an individual who didn't try the sport until I was on the wrong side of 40, I had the dubious distinction of being the oldest person enrolled in the surf school. Call it a mid-life crisis if you will, but it was something which I'd always wanted to do and living on Australia's famous Manly beach meant I had no excuse not to try.

My first stop was one of the many surf shops. Not being young, blonde and beautiful, I was totally ignored by the young sales assistant when I inquired about the wide range of wetsuits available. When beckoned, he reluctantly came over and asked:

'Is it for your daughter?'

This did nothing to build customer rapport! I calmly informed him that it was for me, so he simply pointed at a rack and I was none the wiser as I left, taking my business with me.

I hesitantly walked into the next store, spotting yet another salesman young enough to be my son, but was delighted to encounter a totally different attitude from this young man. He knew and explained his product, gave me some wetsuits to try on and was genuinely helpful. When I emerged from the fitting room to inquire if I had the right size, he thankfully didn't burst into fits of laughter and assured me it was OK.

By this time, he had acquired enough information to know that I wasn't familiar with the surf and was conscious of both warmth and safety. So he suggested that I also purchase some flippers to give me more strength in the water while I learned to body surf. He then asked:

'You don't want to lose them, do you?' An obvious question. I replied in the negative and found myself purchasing ankle straps. As I was about to pay for these three purchases, he added:

'You look like a fun sort of lady and we've got a sale on boogie boards.'

I laughed and replied:

'Thanks, but I think this up-selling (of which he was a master) has gone too far.'

(But guess who now owns a purple and yellow boogie board!)

Handing him my credit card, having spent a small fortune when I simply wanted to buy a wetsuit, I jokingly asked: 'So, what else does a middle-aged surfie chick need?'

With a huge smile, he winked and replied: 'A middle-aged surfie bloke!'

This stereotyped surf shop salesman, complete with long blond hair in a ponytail, earring and dolphin tattoo, had personality plus. He was a marked contrast to his counterpart in the first shop. Both places had the same basic product and the sales staff looked the same, but the service was astonishingly different.

About a year after I became more comfortable on the boogie board, I thought I'd try an actual surfboard and it doesn't take a rocket scientist to know that I returned to the second shop!

It's a pity that the salesperson in the first shop had not been able to suspend his traditional thinking about the needs and wants of the customer. That great ocean of truth that you can't make assumptions about customers remained undiscovered before him and he was unprepared to abandon his traditional thinking about middle-aged women consumers. He was unprepared to be open and ready for the next wave of change because he didn't understand that:

'You can't discover new oceans until you have the courage to lose sight of the shore.'

30

'Life works out best for those who make the best of the way life works out.'

Catherine DeVrye

Ever had one of those bad hair days? Or weeks? Or months? We all do and on those occasions we often think we're the only people in the world who feel that way.

People often ask me, as a motivational speaker, how I stay motivated myself. I tell them that I read and listen to uplifting books and audios, take time to exercise and meditate in nature, have inspirational sayings on the fridge and bathroom mirror, and talk with trusted friends with whom I'm blessed. I then confess that, even with these strategies, there are still days when I too get down in the dumps.

Most people are surprised to learn that I'm not always 'up'. They visualise me on stage, always bright and bubbly, flying around the world, staying in five-star hotels, socialising with interesting people. All that's true. But they forget that I sometimes spend endless hours in an airport waiting for a delayed flight or lost luggage, ending up in the smoking section of a restaurant or alone in an empty hotel room. Because, after the applause and adoration of the crowd has died down, I'm often missing family and friends. It's at times like these that I have to remind myself of the wisdom of this saying, silently repeating—almost as a mantra—that things work out best for the people who make the best of the way things work out. I then approach every 'challenge' more calmly, focusing on what I can do in the given situation rather than getting overly stressed about events over which I have no control.

I haven't always believed this, even though my mother always used to say something similar:

'Things always work out for the best, dear.'

As I last saw her in hospital, dying without dignity, tubes protruding from her frail, cancer-ridden body, I thought of her words and couldn't for the life of me see how things could ever work out for the best again in my life. It was two days before Mother's Day in 1973.

Exactly 25 years later, I found myself about to address an International Year of the Oceans conference. Jean Michel Costeau, son of the renowned Jacques, was the other speaker. A helicopter lifted us from the front of the luxury Vancouver hotel to spectacular views over Howe Sound and Whistler Mountain. It was hard to believe I was the same person who had dejectedly left that hospital room when my Mum had drawn her last breath, so soon after my father had also died of cancer the year before. I remember thinking that my life was over.

In some ways, it was just about to begin, in a totally different direction. As an only child, feeling frightened and alone, I was faced with two choices. I could wallow in self-pity and resort to drugs or alcohol to numb the pain. But that would not bring them back and there was little point in looking backwards. After many tears, I chose to look forwards and make the best of a bad situation. I still had no faith in my mother's words that things always work out for the best. After all, mothers around the world probably resort to that cliché to comfort their kids when they can't think of anything else to say.

In hindsight, I have to admit that there's a lot of truth in that cliché. But I also firmly believe that we need to progress one step beyond those words. Things won't work out for the best unless we take some personal actions and responsibility for making them work for the best.

I have one close friend who is a true inspiration and always great fun to be with. Even though he's never been able to walk without crutches, he travels the world and brings joy to the world around him. Another friend has faced more than her fair share of adversity but even in her darkest moments, her laugh can light up an entire room and you can't help but laugh with her and be pleased to be around her. As we walked along a beach one day, I told her about my conversation with Costeau about the depletion of marine environment, when my thoughts suddenly flashed back to my mother's early pearls of wisdom. Whenever a teenage romance would wane, she'd always say:

'Don't worry, there's lots of fish in the sea, dear.'

Today, there isn't an endless supply of fish, but the literal translation of that school of thought still stands the test of time, with the implication that we always have more options than we think when confronted with events which we would otherwise not choose. So when we have those bad hair days that life inevitably throws in our path, it's imperative to remember that:

'Life works out best for those who make the best of the way life works out.'

31

'Make your life worth living as your living is being made.'

Catherine DeVrye

Think back on people you have known, outside immediate family and friends, who have contributed in some way—large or small—to making your life more pleasant. As you're remembering, it's likely you'll realise that they gave you something but it is unlikely that what they gave you was anything material. It's more probable that they gave you laughter, a shoulder to cry on, a boost in self-confidence or insight into yourself or others. They gave of their time and of their love.

It could have been an encouraging teacher, a boss who believed in you, an acquaintance whom you confided in, a maiden aunt who expanded your horizons, a colleague who willingly helped on a project even though it wasn't their job to do so.

It could even have been a complete stranger—a burly truck driver who, in spite of a tight schedule, stopped to change a tyre for a stranded motorist; a busy service station attendant who carefully gave directions even though you didn't buy anything or were likely to ever return; an insurance agent who called a widow long after her husband's death, just to check she was OK. It could have been a mobile phone dealer who loaned his own phone to a small businessman relying on communication to survive, or a manager who arranged childcare for a single mother in need of an operation.

It might have been the chemist who delivered a prescription to a pensioner after hours at no charge, the doctor who called to follow up the day after an appointment, the florist who, when discovering the patient had left hospital early, took the extra step to deliver the bouquet to their home.

After all, none of us is really in the transport, insurance, retail or health care business. We're all in the people business! And it's been well proven that people prefer to buy goods and services from those they like. In every one of the instances mentioned, repeat business flowed to the person who went that little bit further. By helping others, we do indeed help ourselves, even if it's just by feeling better about ourselves. As Zig Zigler says:

'If you help enough other people get what they want, you'll get what you want.'

When we think of helping occupations, our minds traditionally race to the caring professions of nursing, social work and emergency workers. But every job has the capacity to combine the head and the heart so we can feel we're both making a difference to our own pockets and filling pockets of need in others through random acts of kindness and beauty.

It's sad that a national poll conducted some years ago, revealed that more than 80 per cent of the North American working population did not enjoy the work they do (*Money, Success and You*, John Kehoe, Zoetic Inc., Toronto, 1990, p. 36).

Automotive magnate, Henry Ford, would not have been among those—he once said that:

'A business that makes nothing but money is a poor kind of business.'

When I first started speaking and writing, I was more interested in making a difference than making a fortune like Henry Ford had. Still, I firmly believed that I could make money *and* make a difference. However, like most small business owners, there were many times when I was plagued with self-doubt. If I was having one of 'those' days when nothing was going right, it was all too easy to lose sight of my mission statement of 'helping others help themselves'. Admittedly, I even occasionally felt sorry for myself until I was reminded of others who were far worse off and then took some action to help them. Don't get me wrong, as I'm certainly no Mother Teresa. I get overwhelmed with workload, sometimes to the point of stressing others close to me, as well as myself. At times like those, I need to step back and remind myself that every day I may have the opportunity to improve lives—but I've got to start with my own by remembering to:

'Make my life worth living as my living is being made.'

32

'When you are faced with a choice and don't make it, that in itself is a choice'.

Catherine DeVrye

Every morning we awake and are faced with the choice of how we'll spend our day and what plans we'll put in place for the days ahead. We may sometimes think that we don't have much say in how our day will be; but in fact, if we think about it, we always do.

Sure, we may feel we 'have' to go to work or 'must' look after the children. As responsible adults, we will likely follow that course of action, but it is important to remember that we do so out of choice. Thankfully, in those instances, it's safe to say we've probably made the right choice.

But choices aren't always right or wrong. It's hard to choose between chocolate ice cream and strawberry cheesecake but if you're dieting, it's best to choose neither!

The right choice today may be the wrong one tomorrow and vice versa. Think of all the choices you might make in an average day. You can choose to set the alarm or not and, if it's the former, in a 24-hour period, you have a choice of 1440 minutes. Even if, like most of us, you arise sometime between 6.00 and 8.00 a.m., you still have 120 choices of which minute to set the clock. You can choose to skip or eat breakfast; or choose cereal, fruit, toast, coffee or whatever. If it's cereal, would you prefer cornflakes or porridge? And, if it's cornflakes, there are over a dozen brands to choose from. Will you have whole milk, skim or soy? With or without sugar?

Which of the many brands of toothpaste will you select? Will you decide to shave or put on makeup? What will you wear when you've got a full wardrobe and still nothing seems suitable? And all this happens before you even leave the house for work! Get the drift?

The average person makes hundreds, or more likely thousands, of subconscious choices in a day . . . and that's not even considering the 'big' issues in terms of choosing a career, partner, house and the decision about whether or not to have children.

But do you ever have trouble choosing? And isn't it often when we're faced with choices that we feel stressed about making the right decision? At times like these, we need to remind ourselves that it's far better than the alternative of not having any choices!

Life is certainly more complex these days and it's likely that if the safety pin was invented today, it would have 28 moving parts, a Pentium chip, two batteries and require servicing twice a year. And there would probably be extensive advertising campaigns to determine which brand we'd choose!

Henry Ford told customers they could have any colour of car they wanted as long as it was black. So much for colour choice in those pioneering days of automobiles! Recently I overheard a woman agonise over whether to have metallic paint on the car and whether her mobile phone should be the same colour! However, if she absolutely needed the vehicle or phone for an essential trip or call, colour wouldn't be a consideration! Likewise, if a man were drowning, he wouldn't care what colour the lifebuoy was.

Choice is indeed a luxury. We should cherish choice and never be overwhelmed by the ever-increasing options available to us. It's important to weigh up the pros and cons of various situations and make choices based largely on logic and occasionally on emotion—and never devoid of intuition. We must never succumb to paralysis by analysis and cite the wide array of choices that allow us to do anything we want as an excuse to do nothing at all! Sometimes we see our path clearly, like a well-lit superhighway as we speed along smoothly in a Ferrari. At other times, we feel like a flat tyre in the middle of a dark, foggy night, on a dirt track, apparently going nowhere.

It's our choice, our lives. And our choices largely determine our lives, so remember that:

'When you are faced with a choice and don't make it, that in itself is a choice.'

33

'The only person who welcomes change is a wet baby.'

Anon

You cried. You got fed. You got cuddled. You cried. You got your nappy changed. You got cuddled. It was so simple when someone else was responsible for even the most basic tasks in our daily lives. And we certainly welcomed the change from a wet bottom to a dry one!

It wasn't long before we no longer wanted anyone to change our clothes, no matter how grubby we may have got playing in a mud puddle. We were soon starting to form our own patterns of behaviour and didn't like it when Mummy or Daddy changed our routine. Most of us didn't want to change neighbourhoods or leave the security of being the big kid at primary school to become a little-known identity at high school.

Our tastebuds preferred certain foods and we were not adventurous enough to change our eating habits unless encouraged to do so by powerful advertising campaigns. Admittedly, we were still flexible and had curious minds searching out new adventures. As pre-schoolers, we had few inhibitions about our creative talents and were willing to try most things. It didn't matter to us if we sang out of tune or coloured outside the lines because we didn't have stringent boundaries of behaviour until someone told us we didn't have any musical or artistic talent. Then it was time to withdraw into our shell.

We didn't have a preconceived notion of how the world should be, although we were learning to respond to adults saying 'yes' or 'no'. As teenagers, we had preconceived notions about most things, especially what was cool and what wasn't. We didn't want to try new things unless peer pressure deemed it socially acceptable. We'd developed set habits—whether it was brushing our teeth or something more annoying! But we had our preferred way of doing things.

As adults, we've become increasingly set in our ways. Even changes that we plan and initiate become sources of stress and distress—moving house, renovating a kitchen, a new hairstyle, changing the registration and insurance on that dream car, meeting or leaving the love of your life. The list of changes in our personal lives is endless.

Of course, there are the never-ending changes in our working environment that we often don't initiate and only seldom welcome. Yet, if we're wise, we ascertain which changes are tolerable, which could be to our benefit and which are intolerable.

An ancient prayer says:

'Give me the strength to change what needs to be changed; the courage to accept what can not be changed; and the wisdom to know the difference.'

Changes don't stop when we become more ancient and retire. Although I know and admire many septuagenarians for their willingness to explore new avenues that would put most 20-year-olds to shame, I know others who have become so set in their ways that they're impossible to budge. And, like a baby, they 'spit the dummy' if they don't get their own way.

Talking to a happily married grandmother about the success of her marriage, she informed me that she'd long ago learned to accept that she couldn't change her husband.

'The only time you'll ever succeed in changing a man is when he's a baby, dear,' she said with a laugh. Naturally, the same could be said of women, as both genders age and resist change without discrimination.

Ageing seems to bring increasing resistance to change. Everything has to be exactly as we've always had it. That's not to say we're totally inflexible and unwilling to change, but it's undoubtedly true that we don't surrender to it as readily as we did when we were babies with wet nappies.

Anthropologist Margaret Mead once said that no one would die in the same world in which they were born. It would be almost impossible to calculate the countless changes in our lives since we drew that first breath. As I was jogging along the beach promenade one sunny morning, I noticed a young mother coming toward me, pushing her daughter in a pram, while headed in exactly the opposite direction a middle-aged woman was pushing her mother in a wheelchair. For just a moment, I sensed a 'connection' between the elderly woman and the toddler, reminding me that for many years our body itself has been changing in ways that we now wish it didn't! And, yes, we hope that it won't get to the stage that someone again needs to change our nappy, because we now know beyond doubt that:

'The only person who welcomes change is a wet baby.'

34

'Whether it is the best of times or the worst of times, it is the only time we have.'

Art Buchwald

Time is the ultimate enemy of us all. Yet how often do we forget to spend it wisely? Rich or poor, no one has more than 24 hours per day.

No sooner have I taken my seat on the evening commuter flight than the woman next to me informs me that she doesn't have enough hours in the day and never has enough time to do all the things she needs to, let alone all the things she wants to.

'I don't know if I'm coming or going,' she exclaims in desperate exhaustion. I know what she means and wonder about her words, ever so familiar.

Are we coming or going?

Are we coming home exhausted and going back to work the same way?

Are we coming unstuck and going to pieces

climbing the corporate ladder or falling into an abyss of lost individuality?

Are we coming to a crossroads or going round in ever increasing circles?

Are we coming up in the world or going down in our own self-esteem?

Are we becoming less becoming or are we becoming what we dreamed of?

Are we busy winning a tender or losing our tenderness?

Are we coming from the core of our existence or going to the outer bounds of anonymous chaos?

Are we coming to terms with who we truly are or going crazy trying to be what others expect?

Are we coming unstuck with our insecurities or going to a position of inner strength?

Are we coming of age or going to die prematurely of stress?

Are we coming to realise that we are indeed going to die?

Are we coming to an abrupt halt or constantly going?

Are we going to be happy or just happy to still be going?

With all this coming and going, when are we going to learn that we're coming apart?

Isn't it time we stopped going crazy and started coming to our senses before it's too late?

After all, as Mr Buchwald says, I needed to remind my travelling companion and myself that:

'Whether it is the best of times or the worst of times, it is the only time we have.'

35

'Life is like a 21-speed bicycle—most of us have gears we never use.'

Catherine DeVrye

In preparation for an unsupported cycle adventure over the Andes, I needed a better bike if I was to have any chance at all of completing the trip. After all, it had been a number of years since I'd cycled and the three gears on my old bike were unlikely to give me the technological advantage I'd need. Having reached the other side of 40, I figured I'd need all the help I could get!

Walking into a local cycle shop, a young salesman asked if he could help.

'What would you recommend for a middle-aged woman wanting to cycle over the Andes?' I asked.

'Well, why don't you bring her in and we can see what we can do,' he replied with a wry smile.

This guy was either very good at customer service or a con man. I discovered it was the former, as he patiently explained the various product options. I eventually decided on a custom-made, hot pink, 21-speed model.

With the best technology available, we now needed to start the logistical preparation for a trip that was definitely outside my normal comfort zone. As plans slowly fell into place with my six fellow travellers, it became evident that there were many similarities to the business challenges some of us were facing at the time.

First, we had set ourselves a goal—which at times seemed to be a rather unattainable one—of ascending over 5000 metres from Argentina to the border of Chile and then heading downhill from the summit to the Pacific Ocean, over 800 kilometres away.

A quick look at the map provided a preliminary plan, one which admittedly seemed somewhat daunting until the overall project was broken down into manageable chunks: estimating how much ground could reasonably be covered each day, planning evening stops and making allowances for inclines and questionable road conditions. A buffer of a few days was allowed for contingencies such as poor weather or breakdowns.

After obtaining visas and security clearances, it was time for the physical preparation. In fact, in some ways, we'd inadvertently started those preparations when we first learned to ride a bike, all those years ago. And, although most of us hadn't cycled a great deal since, the basic skills—like many we humans possess—lay dormant and it was no longer necessary to get out the training wheels. We just had to get out of our comfort zones.

We knew that our ageing muscles would have to be eased into a training regime rather gently, so we started with easy rides on a cycle path, without the hazard of cars. Over a period of months, we set a schedule of increasingly longer and more difficult rides, progressing to hills and out on the road in preparation for riding in Buenos Aires traffic (although nothing could have adequately prepared us for that!). With only a few weeks to go, we added to the load by putting telephone books in our saddlebags to condition ourselves to the extra weight. Just like a business plan, we needed to walk before we could run.

Occasionally, in bad weather, we'd use stationary bikes at the gym, but that seemed less motivating as we were busy pedalling and going nowhere and it was harder to remain encouraged without actually feeling you were making some progress. Sometimes it seemed that way as well in my newly formed business! And I occasionally wondered whether I should maybe have a partner, like a partner on a tandem bike, but decided I didn't want to risk the equivalent of doing all the pedalling at the front while someone coasted pleasantly behind.

As the weeks and months rolled on, I surprised myself with increased fitness levels and the enjoyment of cycling with a couple of good friends—the best part was a stop at the end for cappuccinos and some tasty treat. Likewise, on a business journey, it's also important to set little rewards for oneself along the way. This is especially true when you feel you're constantly pedalling uphill or into a headwind.

Like most people starting a new venture or adventure, we'd had a few disagreements leading up to our departure, but these were now behind us as we set off to the airport full of unbridled enthusiasm.

Confidence waned when our bikes arrived damaged and our leader left his passport and saddlebags behind on the very first day. Our tyres and spirits were both flat but we hadn't come this far to give in so easily. He seemed unworried and cheerfully said that there was no use worrying about something he couldn't do anything about so he'd make the most of what he did have. Another good lesson.

After nine hours of an uphill battle against gale-force winds, we wondered if we'd made a serious mistake, but as we hadn't seen a single vehicle in that entire time, there was no choice but to continue to our evening's destination. If we stopped pedalling, we'd fall over. Arriving sore and dirty, we wondered whether we should have trained more rigorously in the first place—and don't we often wonder that about many everyday projects as well! It was also one of those moments when you wished you were at home in your own comfortable everyday environment, but yet knew that, if you'd been there, you'd have been wishing you were off on an exciting adventure! I consoled myself that I was glad I was healthy enough to be able to experience this much temporary pain through my own choice!

The next day or two seemed easier and we worked more as a team, gaining marginal relief from the winds by riding close together in each other's slipstream, with the front rider providing some protection from the fierce environmental conditions over which we had no control. So too, in the economic environments we often find ourselves in, solid partnerships can provide some buffer during particularly bleak times. When we encountered 80 kilometre per hour head winds and snow, our goal seemed impossible. But, through persistence, we found ourselves, a few days later, at the border of Argentina and Chile at the top of the summit pass.

'Why would anyone in their right mind want to cycle over the Andes anyway?' you might ask.

Customs officials must have thought the same thing and body-searched us for drugs, as they were convinced we 'loco gringos' (crazy foreigners) had to be on them! But the rush we felt as we started heading downhill was a natural high, as we easily covered twice the daily distances we had on the ascent, now taking time to stop and enjoy the magnificent scenery.

In the same way, many people think others with innovative ideas are crazy—until the ideas work! We'd done it. We'd stepped outside our comfort zones and tested our own limits. As we philosophised, while dwarfed by magnificent mountains, we couldn't help but be reminded that we were all only part of a much bigger picture and often lost perspective about minor roadblocks in our way. One of my friends, who was having hassles within the large organisation where she worked, commented:

'Well, I got my rear into gear and if I can endure the discomfort of a sore backside while cycling over the Andes, I can easily cope with the people at work who are a pain in the butt!'

There would be no more back-pedalling for her and the brakes were well and truly off as she returned to embark on a new mid-life career with renewed vigor.

So how do ordinary, middle-aged people cycle over the Andes? Exactly the same way we should all approach challenges in our everyday life—one pedal at a time; one step at a time; one distance at a time as we set higher challenges for ourselves than anyone else would. And always remembering that:

'Life is like a 21-speed bicycle—most of us have gears we never use.'

36

'The six most expensive words in business today are: "We've always done it that way!"'

Catherine DeVrye

How often do you hear those words around your organisation? Wasn't it only last month that a senior manager blocked a new employee's suggestion with that exact phrase, adding: 'You just don't understand how we do things around here.' Or, worse still: 'We tried it that way once and the guy who suggested it is no longer here.'

If all this sounds overly familiar, it's time to seriously examine the way in which your organisation operates in today's rapidly changing environment. Certainly, it's important to build on your past successes and not simply change for the sake of change, which is a costly exercise in itself. But never forget that, even if you don't change, your competitors and customers may.

Too often, people confuse necessary change with change for the sake of change. That is not to say that you throw out the baby with the bath water, but any organisation—regardless of its past success—should always remain open to new ideas. It's a recipe for disaster to continue to do things the same old way without at least occasionally assessing if that mode of operation is actually working or you simply *think* it's working for you.

Past success is no guarantee of future success. Of the Fortune 500 companies at the turn of the century, only three exist in their present format today. And, since 1986, only 46 per cent of the Fortune 500 companies are still in business. When management guru Tom Peters wrote *In Search of Excellence* back in 1982, he applauded companies that were innovative, quality focused and growing exponentially. Today, many of them are no longer in business, when not all that long ago, they were considered invincible!

Take a look at a computer company that dominated the world for generations. IBM had incredible market share, rising stock prices and amongst the highest-paid employees in the world. When I did my sales training with them in 1982, we were told that only three computer companies would be in existence by the turn of the century. Never was it considered even a remote possibility that IBM might not be one of them.

It was widely agreed that personal computers were only a fad and wouldn't be a serious contender in the market of the future. And customers would always buy IBM because they'd always bought IBM!

Yet, in the mid-1980s, the share price fell from US$142 to US$42 and over 200 000 employees left the business of the once-invincible company.

Meanwhile, a little backyard company—Apple—was on the rise and seemed to be the new force in the PC business of the early 1990s. Yet Apple's share performance has also fluctuated. Both Apple and IBM are excellent organisations, but change happens particularly quickly in information technology. Fortunately, IBM adapted and, at the time of writing, I'm pleased, as a shareholder, to report their shares are performing well. But no high-tech organisation will even have a parking place on the superhighway (or superhypeway) of the future unless they constantly look at new ways of doing things.

This applies not just to computer companies, but to every organisation, as technology—among other factors—continues to have an ever-increasing influence on the way business is conducted, both domestically and internationally. Can you afford to be complacent that the Internet will have no impact on *your* business?

To succeed, enlightened managers will always look at better ways to run their organisations and hopefully will always remember:

The six most expensive words in business today are: 'We've always done it that way.'

37

'Winners never quit and quitters never win.'

Vince Lombardi

The legendary coach of the Green Bay Packers was also noted for his comment that: 'Winning isn't everything. It's the only thing.' The latter saying may be applicable within the confines of a football locker room, but the former is more relevant to the bigger game of life. We all like to be seen as winners, but not everyone is willing to make the necessary commitment to be one.

As Jeremy Bingham, former Lord Mayor of Sydney, chastises me when I miss triathlon training:

'You've got commitment without the c!'

He's absolutely right in that people who omit, and don't commit, aren't likely to achieve their goals and although my travel schedule prevents me from attending official team training, I assure him I'm still committed to regular exercise.

In sport, and most areas of human endeavour,

it is nothing less than commitment and consistent performance that identifies those who succeed. The eventual winner is not hesitant to put in the additional hours or go the extra distance. They exercise not only their bodies, but also self-discipline to persevere, often against incredible odds. Games aren't won or lost in a packed stadium during the course of a few hours. They are won or lost depending on the effort expended in training year after year, week after week, day after day of hard practice, before one even gets near the big game. It's the same at work. In short, winners do what losers didn't.

A coach, whether on the field or on the shop floor, helps players to monitor progress as objectively as possible. They keep score, readily praise individual success and provide immediate and constructive feedback on areas requiring improvements in performance along the way. It's hard to imagine getting excited about a game with no score, but how often do we expect employees to do so, when they're getting no feedback as to whether they are or aren't kicking corporate goals—unless it's in the form of a kick in the pants.

Achievers need to be made to feel like heroes and a healthy ego, whether dormant or bordering on arrogance, is not uncharacteristic of leaders in sport and business. Only through this inner belief in the intrinsic value of themselves and their goals are they able to motivate others to follow.

That's not to say that leaders are always highly motivated themselves, as everyone has 'down' days.

The difference between winners and losers is that winners lose more often because they're willing to take more risks.

Sport forces athletes to make instant decisions and accept the consequences of their actions. Confidence increases with every victory, however small. Only practice, combined with elements and assessments of success and failure, can develop the intuitive decisiveness and timing that are critical success factors in sport and business alike. The winning manager will provide opportunities for individuals to try new skills and perfect old ones.

They will provide an organisational framework that will help the team reach peak performance rather than succumb to bureaucracy burnout. Policies and hierarchies of organisations do not change overnight, and neither do the rules of a game. The team which eventually wins is unlikely to have expended effort rewriting the rule book; instead, it has probably remained focused on obtaining maximal leverage for its own advantage, through careful interpretation of those rules. A key difference between competition in sport and business is that there is no set time limit in business and the opposition always has time to catch up and render defeat if sustained effort is not maintained!

The score on the board is the bottom line in business. The arena is the marketplace and little can be gained from blaming a spate of industrial injuries for poor performance. Justifications may be valid, but ultimate responsibility rests with the individual leader who must accept and place such situations in perspective and continue moving towards the ultimate long-range goals, in spite of setbacks along the way. As Margaret Thatcher once said: 'You may have to fight a battle more than once to win it.'

Whether one agreed with her policies or not, few would label the former British Prime Minister as a quitter. Most politicians are quick to embrace photo opportunities with sportsmen and women and liberally sprinkle speeches with sporting references such as 'team player', 'game plan' and 'move the goal posts'. Many business leaders also know, whether they've played sport or not, that there are many similar success factors, one of which is that:

'Winners never quit and quitters never win.'

38

'When a door closes, look for a window.'

Catherine DeVrye

We've all had doors slam in our face, literally and figuratively—a big impregnable barrier immediately in front of our eyes that blocks our planned path. At times like this, it almost feels like we're trying to push a sumo wrestler the opposite direction in a revolving door.

Wouldn't there be a greater likelihood of escaping whatever imaginary trap of daily living we find ourselves in if we looked for a totally different approach to whatever the problem is at hand?

Anyone who has ever lost his or her job feels the immediate impact of the employment door closing in their face. In most cases, it's an emotionally draining experience whether you've been dismissed for poor performance or a personality clash with the boss, for which you had some responsibility, or lost your job as part of a downsizing, takeover or bankruptcy, for which you probably had no responsibility.

There are understandable mixed feelings of shock, dismay, insecurity, anger, inadequacy, hurt, persecution, doubt, hopelessness, etc. More surprisingly, over time, many individuals look back on the experience and say it's the best thing that ever happened to them.

'I'd been in a rut for years but never even thought there was anything else I could do.'

'I never really fitted in with their corporate culture anyway and am much happier in my new job.'

'I hate to admit it but I guess the new technology had passed me by because I didn't make the effort to keep up.'

'The payout gave me the opportunity to start the business I'd always dreamed about.'

'That jerk had no right to fire me so I decided to teach him a lesson by going into competition with him. I didn't think we'd make it at first but we now have a higher market share.'

'I never finished school so decided to take an adult education class because I'd always been interested in building.'

Certainly, not everyone finds fulfilment after the devastation of a job loss, but it's important to remember that there are always more choices than we realise if we're willing to think about those other options that are available to us.

Most managers also find it extremely stressful to fire or retrench staff, especially if the person is a good employee. As a human resource manager with IBM, it was some consolation to speak to counterparts in other companies and learn that many employees were, in fact, relieved after the initial shock. They had realised for some time that they weren't up to the job or that the company was in crisis.

Soon after IBM had offered redundancy—mainly voluntary—to 200 000 staff around the world, I saw a t-shirt that read:

'When one door closes, another opens . . . but the passageways are sure hell!'

For some IBM employees, new doors had opened before they even finished their final day at Big Blue. Others who expected flowing offers of employment or consultant opportunities were bitterly disappointed that none were immediately forthcoming. Over time, some colleagues found other great career opportunities in the information technology industry, while others are much happier growing avocados—or, in my case, helping people grow.

I know the transition is easier for those who take a voluntary redundancy or find all of their workmates in the same position of retrenchment. But, even during those tough passageways that we all experience, whether it be between jobs, between relationships or between periods of good health, it's important to remember, even in our darkest moments, that there are probably a lot more alternatives to the problem than we would ever imagine possible.

If we take the time to think about it, we may be amazed at the array of alternatives to our employment, our relationships and our healthcare. When things are going smoothly, we never take any time to reassess. That's why it can be useful to look at those dark passageways not as a source of bleak despair, but rather as an opportunity to see things differently. Rather than focus on what is immediately before your eyes, look creatively towards an unanticipated source of light—possibly from some as yet unexplored avenue of opportunity.

Inevitably, doors *will* close from time to time, and that's the ideal time to look at alternative solutions. Because one is likely to emerge if you can keep in mind that:

'When a door closes, look for a window.'

39

'Whether serving customers or tennis aces, keep your eye on the ball.'

Catherine DeVrye

I've watched and played countless hours of tennis and, whether it is Wimbledon, the Australian Open or the local court, I've never once seen a player win a match by looking at the scoreboard. Champions keep their eye firmly focused on the ball and let the scoreboard take care of itself. Yet how often are we so busy measuring customer satisfaction results and looking at the scoreboard of tangible indicators that we take our eye off the actual customer situation? A classic example was an attempt to improve train service. Although there were indeed improvements in terms of trains running on time, it was also revealed that they weren't stopping at all stations to pick up the passengers, as the drivers were only focused on the measurement of timeliness! So much for keeping your eye on the ball!

Let's look at the acronym of the word 'service'

and other such analogies between service in tennis and service to customers.

Self-esteem

Too often, we confuse service with subservience and people in service jobs don't have the high self-esteem that their roles deserve. How often have you played doubles with someone who ducks and calls out 'Yours'? How often do you work with individuals who do an equivalent 'duck' and call 'yours' when there's a tricky customer situation? We need to feel useful and be able to step up to every customer situation, difficult or otherwise, take ownership of that moment, and call out 'Mine'.

Exceed expectations

As customer demands increase, we need to constantly meet and exceed their expectations. We can never take customers for granted. It's not always the number one seed who wins Wimbledon but often the up and coming players who are willing to go that little extra distance to gain a slight competitive advantage. The same applies in business—and no matter how great a champion you or your organisation may be, success in the past is no guarantee of success in the future.

Recover

We all know that things go wrong from time to time, and even customers appreciate this fact. Encouragingly, the research shows that if you satisfy a customer complaint, and do so quickly, the majority of those customers will become more brand loyal to your organisation if they feel you've adequately recovered from an initially unsatisfactory situation. Just like missing a first tennis serve, most customers let you have a second chance. It's equally important to remember that 96.7 per cent of unhappy customers never take time to complain, so you better not double fault on those who do.

Vision

It's not only essential to keep your eye on the ball, but to keep in mind a long-term vision in order to successfully win tennis games or customer loyalty. Neither happens overnight so, in order to maintain a key competitive advantage, keep in mind a long-term vision. Tennis games aren't won or lost on centre court. They're won or lost on the back courts—hour after hour, day after day, week after week, month after month, year after year of practice.

Improve

Even if we never reach centre court, our tennis game can improve through practice. The difference between an amateur and a professional tennis player is that an amateur will practise until they can get something right. A professional will practise until they never get it wrong. We need to be professional in our approach to servicing customers, as consistency is a key retention factor.

Care

If you're a tennis coach, you care about your players, just as a service provider must care about the needs and wants of their customers. Customer care should never be some phony platitude, but a genuine, heartfelt desire to help the customer by placing yourself in their shoes, whether they are sneakers or high heels! If you like your job and look for daily opportunities to do this, you'll find it easier to succeed. It's better still if you love your job and love helping people. In tennis, love is nothing. In life, it's everything! And it's important that we genuinely care about serving our customers, our organisations, families, communities, planet and ourselves—not necessarily in that order.

Empower

We all like to feel that we can make a difference to the final score; that we're a valued team player; that we can be empowered to stretch ourselves beyond previous personal bests. John Akers, former CEO of IBM, once said:

'If you always get your first serve in, you're not trying hard enough.'

Certainly, it's not all strawberries and cream in the world of customer service, but it will be game, set and match to those individuals and organisations who recognise that looking after customers will result in increased net profits, without you even having to jump the net in victory.

Love all. Love all customers. The ball is truly in your court so remember that:

'Whether serving customers or tennis aces, keep your eye on the ball.'

40

'Success is having what you want and wanting what you have.'

Catherine DeVrye

Do you know anyone who has all the material trappings of success yet never seems to be happy? They've paid off the mortgage and want a bigger house or a bigger office and feel that a gold credit card no longer carries the same status as a platinum one?

Do they really derive pleasure from these possessions or do their possessions possess them?

They own every conceivable toy but have lost all playfulness. They eat at the right restaurants but nothing feeds their inner soul. They fly first class but always put themselves and their families second. They drive a prestige car and never question what drives them. Their bank balance is healthy but their mental and physical health is out of balance. They're recognised in public but seldom recognise their own feelings or those of others close to them.

Hey, don't get me wrong. I'm a firm believer in having nice things myself and don't for a minute think that financial success and happiness need to be mutually exclusive. But it is important to maintain perspective and balance between the material and the spiritual.

It's also important to understand whether you see your glass as half empty or half full. Positive people will see the glass as half full and potentially becoming fuller, whereas negative ones always fear it's half empty and getting emptier. They'll always look at what tasks they dislike in their work, rather than what they enjoy, and what faults their partner has rather than the positive attributes that attracted them to that person in the first place.

The 'grizzle-guts' of this world never seem to be happy, no matter what their circumstances. You readily spot these people with perpetual pouts and frowns when you're the first car stopped at an intersection and you see them crossing in front of you, stooped shoulders, downturned lips and furrowed brows. Rather than being thankful for what they do have, they always want more, more, more. They never know when enough is enough and don't fully appreciate the abundance in their lives because they're too busy counting their cash instead of their blessings. They know the price of everything and the value of nothing, and can no longer enjoy joy for its own sake.

They invest in the stockmarket but not in themselves or their relationships. Some live beyond their means only to impress the folks next door and don't realise that a life dependent on credit cards is of little credit to themselves.

As H. Jackson Brown, author of *Life's Little Instruction Book* says: 'Success is getting what you want and happiness is liking what you get.'

Dr Richard Carlson, renowned psychologist and author of *Don't Sweat the Small Stuff–It's All Small Stuff* puts another slant on the same philosophy:

'One of the most pervasive and destructive mental tendencies I've seen is that of focusing on what we want instead of what we have.'

These modern-day philosophers have thoughts not unlike those expressed prior to 1692, when the *Desiderata* was first discovered. The words of wisdom written then are just as profound today:

'Do not compare yourself with others or you will become vain and bitter because always there will be greater and lesser persons than yourself.'

In a nutshell, they're all saying basically the same thing. To have what it takes to be happy, we need to be happier with what we already have because:

'Success is having what you want and wanting what you have.'

41

'Smiles are passports through deserts
and visas to all foreign countries.'

Robert Darrah

Travelling over 500 000 kilometres per year, I have
more than enough opportunity to pass through customs inspections and, more importantly, to inspect
first hand the customs of various countries around
our planet.

World trade is no longer the exclusive domain
of multinational corporations because technology
has opened up new avenues to provide individuals
with access to other far-away markets.

With billions of dollars per day now passing
across invisible borders, as a result of electronic
commerce, it's easy to forget the huge diversity of
cultures around the globe.

At the start of the new century—and the
millennium—the words 'globalisation' and 'multi-
culturalism' still weren't in my computer's spell
check and a large percentage of the world simply

pays lip service to the benefits gained from cultural diversity.

I'm often appalled at the arrogance and ignorance of Western travellers who try to make themselves understood in a foreign country by raising their voices and becoming angry that they are not understood. It's more important to remember that you are a guest in another country. Just as you'd expect most people to be able to speak the language of your country when they are visitors, isn't it both unreasonable and hypocritical that you also expect them to understand you when you are in their homeland?

Admittedly it's frustrating not to be understood, and we're certainly not all linguists, but it's usually possible to travel around the world without an interpreter (apart from obvious business transactions) if you smile, remain patient and become adept at charades or drawing simple childlike stick pictures to communicate.

It's imperative to remember that, just because people don't speak English, they certainly are not stupid and it's important not to be patronising of other cultures.

Certainly there are different value systems in different countries, and some may be more spiritualistic than materialistic, but these don't need to be mutually exclusive.

One very trendy US clothing designer was reported in a business magazine as referring to Asians as 'monkeys'. Apart from the obvious racist and politically incorrect comments, that's just dumb business in terms of alienating himself from a huge market. And, even though I'm Caucasian, I will no longer buy his products, as a matter of principle.

The more I travel, the more I realise that people are the same. There are distinct differences in ways of doing business and cultural sensitivities. But there are more similarities between people than differences.

They share similar hopes and fears. Basically, everyone wants to simply get on with living, to have a good life for their families, to do their best, to gain job satisfaction and enough money to enjoy their leisure.

At work, they share the same frustrations of not enough hours in the day, too much bureaucracy, internal politics, computers that break or mobiles that are out of range. And, even if they've never heard of a mobile, they're still subject to changing conditions in their external environments over which they have no control—whether they be trade sanctions or floods which wipe out their annual crop.

I've been nervous about speaking to audiences in India, Korea, Indonesia—even Edinburgh or Fort Collins, Colorado. Will they have the same sense of humour as the participants in Sydney? Will my thoughts be relevant? Inevitably, my business fears are allayed, in spite of being served marinated eel for breakfast and noting that the in-flight magazine is in a totally different language! The world is shrinking while our horizons are expanding—if we allow them to.

Whether it is a toothless smile from an old man at the base of the Great Wall of China, or the pearly whites of an eight-year-old child in Kenya, I am constantly reminded of the universality of the human race.

My grandfather used to tell me as a little girl:

'A smile is a frown turned upside down.'

His only travel was when he migrated from Scotland to Canada in 1911. He would marvel at the changes in the world, but one thing hasn't changed, in that apart from war-torn lands:

'Smiles are passports through deserts and visas to all foreign countries.'

42

'Remember yesterday. Plan for tomorrow. Live for today.'

Catherine DeVrye

We all know people, in our professional and personal lives, who spend most of their time looking back on the good old days and wishing for their return. We also know others who are so busy dreaming and planning for tomorrow that they will never be happy with what's happening today.

Most of us were brought up to learn from the past and plan for the future. Living for the moment was certainly seen as somewhat irresponsible in our house. Mum told me to learn from experience and Dad worried about providing for the future. He looked forward to retirement but never had a chance to enjoy it because he died of cancer the very first year. I only remember him having one holiday. After all, work was the responsible thing to do.

I'm not, for a moment, advocating that we don't consider the consequences of our actions today. Nor am I suggesting that we don't also learn from the past. But we do need to take time to enjoy the present. When I was diagnosed with a malignant melanoma, I thought of my father. It reminded me not only of the fear of dying, but the fear of not living as I wanted. It was in some ways a wakeup call to strike a better balance between learning from the past and planning for the future.

It had been a long time since high school, when I first heard the maxim: 'Today is the first day of the rest of your life.'

I have no idea who first uttered those words of wisdom that I haven't always lived by. I couldn't wait to leave high school. Then I looked forward to completing university, but unlike some people—who never enjoy the moment—I certainly had fun along the way!

I'd been taught to postpone gratification—that the good things (like dessert) were worth waiting for. But some people carry that philosophy to extremes, always hoping that 'someday' will be better than today. Those people are unlikely ever to be happy.

Alternatively, others are spendthrifts with their money and their time. They spend like there is no tomorrow, being irresponsible with emotions and actions and totally ignoring the future consequences of their present behaviour. We all know individuals who say 'When I graduate, then I'll be happy.' 'When I get married, then I'll be happy.' 'When I lose some weight, then I'll be happy.' 'When I get that promotion, then I'll be happy.' 'When the mortgage is paid, then I'll be happy.' 'When the kids have left home, then I'll be happy.' 'When I retire, then I'll be happy.' When, when, when. Then, then, then. Then they die, having seldom been happy. That idyllic someday never arrived.

It's still possible to remember yesterday and plan for tomorrow while living for today—truly living. Understand that time stands still for no one and some things just won't wait. As you're finishing a day's work, the sunset won't wait until the computer is turned off; the beauty of a rainbow will be gone in a moment; your child's first steps won't be postponed until you're home from that business trip.

I wish I knew who originally said something along the lines of:

'Yesterday's history. Tomorrow's a mystery. All we have is today, and it's called the present, because it is indeed a gift.'

A few have claimed credit for these words of wisdom, but who knows? All I do know is that we must indeed seize the day and:

'Remember yesterday. Plan for tomorrow. Live for today.'

43

'The road to hell is paved with good intentions.'

William James

Whether we postpone unpleasant tasks, or postpone our own happiness, procrastination seldom furthers our future benefit. Handle that piece of paper only once. Take the kids to the beach before the weather changes. Do the most important things on your 'to do' list early. Make that call to a sick friend before it's too late. Get those unpleasant tasks out of the way as soon as possible. They won't get any easier by haunting you. Do it *now*.

I was always guilty of leaving university assignments until the last moment and struggling with my final thesis was no exception. I'll never forget when Dr Wally Schwank, the Dean of the University of Montana graduate school, called me into his office and sat me down. I was feeling more than a little negligent and worried he was going to chastise me for partying too much at the expense of my studies. Much to my surprise, he then handed me the most glowing letter of reference I could imagine.

'Wow, thanks,' I stammered.

Sternly, he replied, his eyes never wavering from mine, 'Now it's time you lived up to it! I'll put it in my drawer for safe keeping until you graduate.'

His words were far more effective than any possible disciplinary action. No wonder he was such an outstanding leader and football coach. I immediately curtailed my social activities and buckled down to study.

Reflecting on those university days of the seventies, I remember talking until the wee hours of the morning about revolutionising the world. Now, we reinvent the corporation or remodel the kitchen. But, whether changing the world or changing the wallpaper, we need to remember that all change must first start with us, as individuals.

We all know those individuals who are 'Gunnas'. They're gunna do this and gunna do that, but they never do. Worst of all is the person who is gunna be happy—one day. They have an unlimited supply of excuses, living their lives with a string of 'what ifs'. What if this? What if that? What if I'd been born taller? What if my parents had been wealthy? What if my boss recognised my talents? What if the company hadn't merged? What if I win the lottery? What if? What if? What if?

The only place for 'what if' analysis is on a spreadsheet, because life isn't about neatly arranged columns and variables that we can predetermine and move around at will. Life isn't about what if, but what *is*.

> *At times we may ask*
> *'What if this? What if that?'*
> *And sometimes we wonder*
> *just where we're at.*
> *But we can't waste our lives*
> *wishing what might have been.*
> *We must live for now.*
> *You know what I mean.*
> *Life isn't perfect,*
> *Of this we are sure.*
> *And sometimes it seems*
> *No more can we endure.*
> *But rather than worry*
> *About what we have not*
> *It's best to count blessings*
> *For all that we've got.*
> *There's no point lamenting*
> *'Why, oh why me?'*
> *Take control of your life*
> *If you want to be free.*
> *If you want a life*
> *That holds far more bliss.*
> *Stop asking 'what if?'*
> *Make the most of what is!*

What if we knew what the future held? That may be good, but what if we learned we only had six months to live? What would we do then? How would we choose to spend our precious present moments on earth? Psychologists suggest that we should ponder what indeed we would do if we only had a short time to live and then make sure we do more of it—every day—to bring more joy to our lives. As that great philosopher, Anonymous, once said:

'Life is not a dress rehearsal.'

Australian media magnate and keen golfer Sir Frank Packer put it another way:

'Life is not a practice round.'

Program time in your diary with things that you want to do before it gets filled with an array of activities that you don't want to do. Make time every day for friends and family and for yourself because, on the balance sheet of life, that time won't carry forward to tomorrow. Yesterday is a cancelled cheque. Tomorrow is an IOU. Today is cash in hand. Spend it wisely to bring more joy to your time on earth. Do it now—if you don't, you'll only regret it later when you discover that:

'The road to hell is paved with good intentions.'

44

'Not everything that is faced can be changed but nothing can be changed until it is faced.'

James Baldwin

The words boldly spoken by a civil rights leader in the 1960s are just as poignant today when we consider not only civil rights but also our individual and collective rights and responsibilities toward customers, colleagues, families, friends, communities and our planet—and, of course, to ourselves. The last responsibility seems the most readily overlooked.

It's far easier not to face up to unpleasant situations, to simply drift along, complain and place the blame squarely on someone else—anyone else. Blame the boss, co-workers, suppliers or the government when all else fails—or your spouse, siblings, parents and teachers. Whether the blame is real or imagined, seldom do we actually directly express our dissatisfaction with a situation; rather, we simply keep complaining to anyone who will listen. Usually it is sympathetic friends, but they too can grow tired of hearing a litany of dissatisfaction with no corresponding action to resolve whatever is causing it.

'My mother didn't give me enough love as a child so I'll never have a happy relationship.'

'No matter what I did, my father never felt it was good enough and it's the same with my boss, so how do you expect me to have a successful career?'

'My teachers never encouraged me so don't talk to me about lifelong learning.'

'All my family is overweight so what's the point of trying to get fit?'

We've all heard such comments. Sometimes we're sympathetic, but more often than not, we're tempted to remind the person that, whether it is because of denial, avoidance or simply refusing to accept responsibility for circumstances, we can never forget that no one else is responsible for our lives except us. Certainly, others may have contributed to the current state of affairs, but unless we face up to the fact that it's up to no one but ourselves to chart the course for our future, only unhappiness can result.

Everyone feels down in the dumps from time to time, sensing that events have got out of control and they're powerless to do anything. But what separates the successful people from the unsuccessful is that successful ones know that most situations, however desperate, are only temporary and the individual is never totally powerless.

What is required is a plan of action to see what, if anything, can be done about a given situation, rather than expend precious energy on what cannot be done to change the past. Sometimes, well-meaning friends aren't enough to conquer whatever demons torment us, and it may be necessary to seek unbiased professional help to face up to the painful emotions inevitably caused by the death of a parent, the breakup of a relationship, or conflict at work. Whether it is a doctor, member of the clergy, psychologist or whoever, there comes a time in everyone's life when it could be beneficial to talk to someone else even if it means swallowing our pride. It's non-fattening and often others with no personal involvement can see a situation in a totally different light. Certainly, there is still a stigma attached to counselling but few of us would hesitate to call in an expert to fix our electric stove or automobile.

And there's something about an 'expert's' guidance that we're often more willing to accept than that of friends. This is possibly because we may have paid for the advice, so therefore place a higher value on it; or possibly because we've reached a more receptive stage by virtue of making the move to seek another perspective to help us make the necessary changes in our lives.

Often, simply admitting that the problem isn't entirely someone else's and there is indeed something which we as individuals can do, is enough to put us on the right path. We may not even fully listen to advice given, but the mere step of talking things through and recognising that the problem is not unsolvable may be enough to get us headed in a different direction. An external influence may be the necessary catalyst for us to make a personal commitment to stop ignoring a festering problem. Sometimes, facing up to one's personal responsibility for the situation is enough to formulate a game plan for change.

That's not to advocate any knee jerk reactions or overnight magical solutions, but rather a series of altered thoughts and behaviours to gradually modify and improve individual well-being for the future.

Endless complaining won't make the difference. Nor will procrastination. As an old Chinese proverb so eloquently points out, the journey of a thousand miles begins with the first step. Whatever situation we wish to change, we've all got to start somewhere, sometime, somehow.

Once we face the fact that we're broke, we can start saving one dollar at a time. Once we face the fact that we're out of shape, we can start by walking one step at a time. Once we face the fact that the house is a mess, we can start by tidying one item at a time. Once we face the fact that we're unemployed, we can start by applying for one job at a time. Once we face the fact that we have a drinking problem, we can start by abstaining one day at a time. Once we face the fact that we're miserable, we can start by smiling one smile at a time. Once we face the fact that we feel unloved, we can start by loving ourselves and others one moment at a time.

Admittedly, it doesn't always work—and certainly not always right away—but admitting and facing the changes we'd like to see happen in our lives is a prerequisite for having any chance of change actually eventuating.

James Baldwin was so right in saying:

'Not everything that is faced can be changed, but nothing can be changed until it is faced.'

45

'The two most under-used words in our vocabulary are "thank you".'

Catherine DeVrye

Call me old-fashioned if you will, but there's little that annoys me more than the absence of a simple thank you. Whether it's face to face, a phone call or a note of appreciation, there's no excuse for bad manners.

'Why do you send presents to one cousin and not the others?' asked a friend.

'I used to send gifts to everyone, but only one ever sent me thank you notes over all those years. It wasn't the money. I just felt that they either didn't like or appreciate the present, so why waste money?'

None of us likes to be taken for granted. I don't expect undying devotion, but I do think it's reasonable to expect a simple thank you.

'Didn't you even send a wedding present?'

No. After eleven years of no correspondence, I

felt no obligation simply because an invitation suddenly arrived in the mail. I knew that she expected a gift, but that expectation was the problem because I'd expected at least an acknowledgment over the years.

What does it cost to say thank you? Not a cent, but it pays long-term dividends. It takes just a second, but the impact lasts much longer. Whether in personal or business relationships, it's so simple to do and so easy to overlook. Take time to say thanks and you'll be thanked many times over.

How many times would we give or receive a thank you in an average day? A cursory thanks for the wakeup call, the person who opens a door for you, hands you a memo, sells you groceries, drives the bus to work?

Whenever I travel to a foreign country, I only need to learn to say thank you in their native tongue. Faces light up and most transactions thereafter can be conducted with a primitive combination of charades, smiles, stick drawings and patience. *Merci, Che che ni, Gracias, Kiaora, Danke, Domo arigato, Terimakasi, Asanti-san.* Whatever the dialect, thank you in any language works wonders.

How often do we overlook thanking someone for a task we've come to expect they'll do? We justify our actions by saying 'that's their job' or 'they've always done that and they know I appreciate it'. Do they?

I'm reminded again of the apocryphal story of a husband who tells his wife on their wedding day:

'I love you but don't expect me to say it all the time. If my feelings change, then I'll let you know!'

Few women (or men) would be satisfied with that lack of expressed emotion from their partner. So too, in any personal or professional setting, we all like to feel appreciated and never tire of receiving a thank you ourselves, as long as it's genuine. We might brush off those two little words with either 'you're welcome' or 'oh, it was nothing'. It's not so much the thank you we remember but the absence thereof!

People like to feel appreciated—to have their assistance recognised. And the sooner the better. It's more effective to praise a child, employee, colleague or friend immediately. Not only will the reason for your appreciation be fresh in their mind, but also in yours. So act now! It's better to do so than make a mental note to say thanks at a later stage and then inadvertently overlook your good intentions.

It could be thanks for a job well done by an employee, a peer who helped you out even though it wasn't officially their job, or even a boss who has offered outstanding support—just as long as your thank you is seen as sincere and not sycophantic. It could be to a supplier who rushed an order or another who never lets you down. It could even be to someone who you are unlikely to have any future contact with, such as a pleasant flight attendant or cheerful toll collector. The more specific your thank you is, the more valued it becomes to the recipient. There's a huge difference between a hurried 'thanks' as you jump out of a taxi or a 'thank you very much for having a clean cab and driving so safely'. Try the latter and just watch the driver's eyes light up. It will make you feel better as well!

Maybe even get in touch with someone who once made a difference in your life a long time ago. A phone call, or a couple of sentences on a postcard, will only take a few minutes in your busy day but it could make someone else's and have an impact which could last their lifetime.

Sure, we don't receive many such letters ourselves and we're all busy, but isn't it worth thinking about—to let someone know you're thinking about their worth because they helped boost your personal stakes along the way?

It's also worth thinking about how 'TGIF' has become part of the 9–5 working vocabulary. Rather than say Thank Goodness It's Friday, wouldn't it be better to say, Thank Goodness It's Monday? Thank goodness phones are ringing. Thank goodness customers are interrupting us. Thank goodness even for the hassles when the computer breaks down or the bank makes an error. Thank goodness I am gainfully employed and have an opportunity to contribute. Few people ever stop to be grateful for their job, but we'd all appreciate it much more if we didn't have one and needed the income. The best way to appreciate your job is to imagine yourself without one!

Most importantly, we should be thankful for everything that we have and remind ourselves at least once a day to say a silent thank you for all the blessings in our lives—even if, at the moment, things might not be working out quite as we planned.

As my head hits the pillow every night, I give thanks for both everything I have and everything I don't have. Paradoxical as that may sound, I'm pleased that I do have a clean bed, a full tummy and a roof over my head. I'm equally pleased that I don't have to close my eyes facing unbearable pain or political persecution. No matter how bad my day has been, I know there's always someone—in fact many people—much worse off than me.

Sometimes, when I'm feeling exhausted and haggard, I need to remind myself that wrinkles don't hurt! Nor would baldness be life threatening! It's so useful to take a quiet moment to reflect and rejoice in the specific things that went right in the day: thankful for close friends and opportunities. Even if alone, far from home, I'm still thankful that I'm able to read, think, talk, laugh and enjoy sunsets. So many of the best things in the world are free if we free our minds long enough to appreciate them, and to appreciate that:

'The two most under-used words in our vocabulary are "thank you".'

46

'We're here for a good time—not a long time!'

Frank Jansen

How do you measure a year in your life?

Most of us greet the New Year, a birthday or other milestone as an annual event. Yet, there are 365 days, 8760 hours, 525 600 minutes and 31 536 000 seconds in that year.

It's important to spend those smaller moments of time wisely. We don't always do so, but it's better to say we wasted a day or learned from the unpleasant experience of the last week than it is to say we wasted a year. Nothing can change the past or allow us to re-live those actual hours, so it's important to live them fully along the way.

I recently received an e-mail that said:

'Always give 100 per cent at work.'

It seemed a noble enough sentiment until it expanded to:

'Give 15 per cent on Mondays, 20 per cent on

Tuesdays, 25 per cent on Wednesdays, 25 per cent on Thursdays and 15 per cent on Fridays!'

Whether it be work or any other area of endeavour, it's important to give 100 per cent to the task at hand. That moment won't come again. When you're working, focus on work and don't waste energy worrying about home. When you're home, enjoy your friends and family and don't lament what happened at the office earlier in the day or what may happen tomorrow. It won't change events, so we might as well keep problems in their proper place and in perspective.

Dr Richard Carlson so aptly said in his book, *Don't Sweat the Small Stuff—And It's All Small Stuff*:

'How much of a problem do we make of our problems?'

Minutes, hours and days can be wasted with worry rather than assessing what we're actually capable of doing at the time and making the most of that moment.

As a motivational speaker, audiences perceive that I'm always 'up' and seem surprised when I confess that some days I feel about as dynamic as a dead sea slug! As much as I'd like to, I don't always have ten out of ten days. If the computer breaks and the technician is unavailable until the next day; if a flight is delayed and I'm stuck at an airport on the other side of the country; or if I have a miserable cold, I know these are all going to be three out of ten days at best! So, rather than stress about the inevitable, I try to make it the best three out of ten day possible.

Rather than worrying about the broken computer, which is admittedly my key business tool, I try to prioritise other non-computer-related tasks. Rather than pacing up and down at the airport, I always carry a good book to read and phone numbers of friends or clients in that city. Rather than cursing the cold, I see what I can do to relieve it and take things easier as my body rests. Admittedly, I'm not always successful with this strategy, but even if I reduce the stress levels in one or two situations, I'm better off than before by having made optimal use of that time.

Time is our most valuable non-renewable resource and I hate wasting time and having others waste mine. People who are perpetually late show no respect for the time of others. Sometimes it's unavoidable to be late, but those who habitually think friends and colleagues have nothing better to do than wait for them show a distinct lack of respect for that relationship. A close friend once chastised me for being late. 'You're almost as bad as so and so,' she said coolly but calmly. I was annoyed. She was right—to remind me. That's what true friends are for. That's the difference between trusted friends, of which I have only a few, and a myriad of pleasant acquaintances. Friends love you even if you're late, or sick, or make a faux paux. They love you in spite of your actions, not only because of your actions and are able to kindly guide you when your actions appear off course. They're there for you in good times and bad.

They're not those annoying people who speak of 'killing time', without realising it is time which indeed kills us all in the end. I've never liked the concept of 'killing time'. That's not to say I don't relish relaxing while watching a sunset, or over a good meal with good friends but those are conscious choices of how I spend my time. I find it strange to grasp the concept of boredom as there is always so much to do, whether it be learning something new or helping someone in need.

Every moment is as fleetingly precious as a drop of water in the midst of a timeless desert. It's important how we ration that non-renewable natural resource towards activities which are important to us, rather than rationalising how we wasted time that can never be recouped. I once did a time management course, which asked a question I'd never forget:

'If you had only six months to live, how would you spend that time?'

I've subsequently asked myself a similar question with slightly different parameters. What if I had only six weeks to live, or six days, six hours or 60 minutes? How would I spend those last precious finite moments? And why aren't I doing more of those things that I'd like to do—now?!

That's not to say that we should be irresponsible, with no thought of tomorrow. But we should make sure that we consciously program time in our busy schedules for what is truly meaningful to us. Otherwise, we'll simply see our calendars fill up with what others think is important, or what we think we should do—thus never having time for what we actually want to do. Dr Stephen Covey has written an entire book on this subject. Titled *First Things First*, it's an excellent read to help focus on making time for the most important things in our life and it offers many valuable lessons.

It is said that time is the best teacher. Unfortunately, it eventually kills even its best students, which is why there's no time like the present to reassess how we spend our time and remember the words of octogenarian Frank Jansen who, many years ago, told me that:

'We're here for a good time—not a long time!'

47

'You can't take care of your customers if you don't take care of yourself.'

Catherine DeVrye

'I'm too busy to exercise. I never seem to have enough time for my family and friends. Who can spare an hour to go to the gym? How can I quietly read a book and listen to music when I've got so much to think about?'

Does this sound familiar? We've all either spoken or heard one of these distressed comments. After all, we've gone to seminars and been told that the customer is number one.

Rubbish! Even as the author of a #1 best-selling book on customer service, I know that customer well-being is not nearly as important as my personal well-being. This may sound selfish and contrary to popular business thinking, but I can't possibly deliver exceptional customer service and serve others to the best of my ability unless I have ample physical and mental reserves myself. We need to *be* at our personal best to *give* our personal best.

If we're at work and feeling guilty about yelling at the kids or not calling our ageing parents, or resentful that we had to forgo a golf game to work on yet another quality certification all weekend, what frame of mind will we be in to greet our customers?

Try as we might, the best customer service providers are only human (apart from the automatic teller machines!) and all humans need to have their batteries recharged. As much as we may genuinely want to give, we cannot do so if we have no reserves from which to draw our energy.

Some daily exercise helps restore the balance. A simple walk will suffice—it doesn't need to be a marathon. And daily means every day! You need not sign up for the Iron Man event, but as far back as the time of Aristotle, the correlation between a healthy mind and healthy body was recognised. You may have even forgotten how good it feels to be well—wellness being not simply the absence of disease, but a feeling of physical and mental well-being.

Often the only treadmill some people are on is the one of constantly working. We're so busy being busy, so tired of being tired, that—like the treadmill—it feels like we're frantically moving but getting nowhere.

As a reformed workaholic, I know that physical and mental relaxation is easier to talk about than do. And it's easier still to get into a vicious circle of working harder in the hope that you will have more leisure time; to get more customers so you can afford that long-overdue holiday.

But if you take better care of yourself, you'll be able to take better care of your customers. In return, they will take better care of your financial needs through repeat business. So please remember that:

'You can't take care of your customers if you don't take care of yourself.'

48

'Life is the biggest and fastest game
of all and when the final score is in,
it's not whether you win or lose that
counts but how you played the game.'

Doc Carlson

This sports leader early in the last century would
never have anticipated the mega-salaries for athletes
today, and a cynic might well choose to re-frame
Carlson's words as: 'It's not whether you win or lose
but how good a lawyer you have to negotiate your
contract.'

Whether one is a basketball star or lawyer,
much of our sporting language and principles are
also applicable to other areas of human endeavour.
After all, we do participate more often than we
actually win.

As General Colin Powell said: 'The healthiest
competition occurs when average people win by
putting in above-average effort.'

Is sport of any more significance to leaders of
armies, nations and corporations than simply a mere
diversion from the main event? Although there is

little quantitative research to substantiate this theory, the answer appears affirmative because of the many traits transferable from the sporting arena to the business forum.

Into his seventies, the founder of Sony, Akio Morita, was still an active golfer, skier and tennis player, and once compared the volatile Japanese money market to a golf game, where holes have a different handicap each day. Morita's friend, John Opel, also used a golf reference when asked if he would do things differently as CEO of IBM at the time:

'All of us would, but I don't carry those things around in my head or it spoils the bigger picture. If you worry about the putt you missed on the third hole, you'll ruin the rest of your game.'

Thousands of successful chief executives in the private and public sectors have proven their competitive skills in formulating successful game plans for their own organisations. It is not surprising that a number of these leaders have been active participants in sport.

This is not to say that those who have not participated in sport will not succeed in business, or that a gifted sportsman or woman will necessarily be good in business. However, there are some commonalities of competition, perseverance, decision-making, team play, leadership and motivation.

A survey of 60 managers attending the Monash Mt Eliza Business School revealed a positive attitude toward sport, and almost 98 per cent had voluntarily participated in sport at some stage. Over 68 per cent had engaged in formal competition, a useful foundation for management where one must constantly compete not only for market share but resource allocation within an organisation.

Competition in sport provides a background for a realistic assessment of the strengths and weaknesses of your opponent and yourself. It instils a belief in reward for effort, the ability and persistence to fight back after a defeat or injury and the importance of critical timing—all traits sought in a manager.

Over two-thirds of managers surveyed cited active participation in team sports. Frequent references are made to management teams in business and the good team player is a valued asset. Such a person recognises that the joint effort is greater than the sum of the parts and strives toward realisation of a common corporate objective, while still seeking individual recognition.

There is acceptance that it is sometimes necessary to hand the ball to someone else, even though you would prefer to score yourself. The expectation is reciprocity in the next play or game. Participation in a sporting team teaches one that help must be given in order to be received.

Almost 7 per cent of managers responded that they had been a sporting coach, and the same percentage registered as a team captain. A manager is a coach of an organisation and must carefully consider a game plan to obtain optimal performance from all positions on the field or on the shop floor. He or she must scout for the basic talent and then nurture skill—both obvious and latent—in every individual player. Pre-game training and post-game analysis must be ongoing and, in addition to those individual components, a coach must cultivate and consolidate an overall team spirit.

Adroit delegation is also critical so each player clearly understands the role expected of them and how it relates to other team members, in order to avoid unnecessary confusion in key situations. In many sports, you must call 'yours' or 'mine' when going for a ball. Likewise, a good manager will communicate precisely to employees what is 'theirs' in terms of responsibility.

They will support risk-taking and encourage employees to test their limits, without taking punitive actions if initial mistakes occur. The person who makes no mistakes in sport or business must simply be sitting on the sidelines and that could be the biggest error of all! That's why it's worthwhile to remember that:

'Life is the biggest and fastest game of all and when the final score is in, it's not whether you win or lose that counts but how you played the game.'

49

'Your key competitive advantage dreams with you every evening and looks at you in the mirror every morning.'

Catherine DeVrye

Is the reflection one that you'd welcome when you wake? It's important to like what we see—not just on the outside, but the reflection of the true spirit of our inner being. We are who we are.

Admittedly, rumpled hair, baggy eyes and toothpaste frothing from our mouth is not always a pretty picture, but look beyond the exterior and like the inner person who looks back at you and through you from that mirror. Believe that, in spite of inevitable obstacles, our hopes and dreams are waiting to be fulfilled when we acknowledge the power of our own individuality.

Too often we are defined, and define ourselves, by what we do. Our external appearance is incorrectly seen as our internal worth.

Following a bank merger, one of the Melbourne offices updated its premises with new fittings and carpet. A long-time, but very dishevelled, customer arrived with his dog as he had done for years. He was informed by one of the new staff that dogs weren't allowed. When he protested and asked to speak to the manager, he received the same rather rude response and the manager seemed totally disinterested when the customer threatened to close his account, as he didn't appear to have two cents to his name. You can imagine the shock when he withdrew over a million dollars, then walked to the bank across the street, where the staff had a totally different attitude and didn't judge a book by its cover.

How many similar stories have you heard of tramps who die with millions in the bank or, conversely, those who led a lifestyle of the rich and famous while on the verge of bankruptcy? It seems that we receive better treatment from service providers if we're better dressed, but to assume that we're higher net-worth customers, based on our appearance, is a fallacy indeed.

Only those who are confident about the core of their being feel totally comfortable in their own skin and have no need to put on airs and graces for the outside world. My personal preference would be to never wear panty hose, high heels and makeup, and I suspect that few men enjoy wearing ties. Yet, it's expected that we dress the part in most business and social situations. If I'm a banker, it doesn't mean that I'm more financially astute because I'm wearing a three-piece suit. But, even if

I was a financial genius, the unfortunate bottom line is that not many customers would choose to trust my judgment if I wasn't dressed the part and met them in shorts and a t-shirt.

As a motivational speaker, I become public property after presentations at conferences. Even on an exercise bike in the gym, attendees have asked questions relating to my talks and what I do. Very few conference attendees get to know who I actually *am*.

On Australia Day 1999, I was speaking in Miami, Florida—about as far from Sydney, Australia as one can get. One of the industry experts at the convention, who hadn't heard my presentation, mentioned a desire to try a Cuban restaurant. My first taste of Cuban food was far from memorable, but it was one of the most pleasant evenings I'd spent having dinner with a stranger. We enjoyed a similar sense of humour, and discussed our dogs, ex-husbands, families, tennis and other sports that wouldn't have normally been on the agenda because we'd have felt obliged to wear our professional hats, representing not only ourselves, but also our organisations and expected image.

It reminded me of a time when I was considering a career change and was admittedly reluctant to leave IBM, as it not only provided a secure salary and many opportunities, but was also considered a prestigious company to work for. How would I feel if I introduced myself without my IBM business cards? How would others react?

On a ski trip, I decided to anonymously test reactions. Under the frosted veil of hat and goggles, riding a chairlift with different skiers every trip, I'd try to judge others' judgment of my proposed career change. The solo skier knows that, during the course of a six to eight minute ride, you usually learn how long your travelling companion has been at the resort, where they're from, what they do for a living and what runs they'd recommend. If you seem of similar skiing ability, you may even head down one run together, with no commitment to making a second.

When the question inevitably came up about occupation, I stuttered what I really wanted to do, rather than what I was actually doing. Without my familiar point of reference, I tentatively tried my new role on for size and it certainly didn't feel comfortable at first. 'I'm an author and speaker,' I mumbled as softly as a snowflake hitting the ground.

People would probably think that was little more than a euphemism for being unemployed. Much to my amazement, there seemed not only a readiness to accept this rather unconventional occupation, but an associated curiosity to learn more.

By the end of the week, I felt more confident to pursue my desired path, but persisted in pursuing the 'What do you do for a living?' game. Interestingly, the response I received—especially from males—was totally different depending on whether I claimed to be a teacher or technician; flight attendant or financier; nurse or nuclear physicist. Laying claim to the latter was a guaranteed conversation stopper until I actually met a nuclear physicist!

It was time to stop my silly game, knowing that it was more important to be defined by who we are than what we do. I now realise that the more important question isn't what we do for a living, but what we do for a life. It's not what we do for a living, but what our living does for us. It's not what we do for a living, but what we live to do. And it's essential that, regardless of what it is that we do, to remember that we must be true to ourselves well beyond what others may see on the surface, knowing that:

'Your key competitive advantage dreams with you every evening and looks at you in the mirror every morning.'

50

'Do what you believe in. Believe in what you do.'

1993 motto of Rotary

As a Rotarian for some years, I only discovered the true meaning of this saying when I started my own business the same year. I've since lost count of the many times in the early days when I doubted my decision to leave the security of the corporate world to venture out on my own. I hadn't appreciated that high overheads and low cash flow seem to be the norm in any start-up business.

Most owners occasionally question whether they have indeed made the right decision. But successful operators chose their particular path because of their original belief in themselves—that they could successfully offer a particularly excellent good or service. Most gave their venture considerable thought, but never thought it would be quite as hard as it was!

It's not at all unusual for self-doubt to rear its

ugly head at a time when you believed you could do it and others believed you were crazy to even try. There's not much point giving the bank manager a copy of Napolean Hill's legendary book *Think and Grow Rich*. The bank manager requires more than thinking to keep him or her happy. But, in that book, Hill points out:

'What the mind can conceive and believe, a person can achieve.'

Admittedly, belief in itself isn't enough. Preparation, hard work and talent are other prerequisites for success. Belief is indeed an essential ingredient, and most successful people (there are exceptions) are truly committed to their course of action and are not easily deterred from inevitable setbacks. Like the childhood story of 'The Little Engine Who Could', it's important to keep telling ourselves:

'I think I can. I think I can'. Or better still:

'I know I can. I know I can,' as we chug along on our journey.

The good news is that most people are quitters, so if we stick to what we believe in, in time we'll be winners. Inner belief in themselves and their course of action is what sustains successful people through difficult times. They feel as if they have a sense of purpose in what they're doing—both to earn a living and to earn the respect of family, friends, community and self.

They hope that if they do what they love, the money will follow and abundance, however they may define it, will become a way of life. Abundance

218

need not necessarily be defined as material possessions. Mother Teresa, although from a wealthy family, chose to serve the poor. Surrounded by poverty, she led an abundant life through doing what she believed in. Most of us can only marvel at her mixture of courage and compassion. We can only guess that, being human, she too may have experienced some times of self-doubt, wondering if that's what she was meant to do, if she was on the right path, if anyone cared, if she would be better—or happier—doing something else.

Millionaire comedian George Burns probably also at first doubted his ability to stand on stage, and wondered if anyone would laugh. That too takes courage of a different sort, but as he said:

'I'd rather be a failure at something I enjoy than a success at something I hate.'

I reflected on his words while waiting to be the after-dinner speaker on the evening of the largest lottery draw in the history of the USA. Conversation around the table speculated about what folks would do if they won the lottery. Most wishful thinkers proclaimed that they'd retire, buy a yacht or a holiday home and travel. They were amazed, but no more so than me, when I said I'd do exactly what I'm doing now (though admittedly with a more relaxed schedule and less paperwork!).

I realised how truly blessed I was in my work—that my passion could also be my profession as it can be for all of us. I recognised that the hard struggle and doubt of the early days was finally paying off. I slowly discovered that making money and making a difference were not mutually exclusive, and met numerous people who had known this all along.

I'm not saying that money isn't important, but whether we play the stockmarket or not, we're all shareholders in the biggest capital asset of all—ourselves! We can never make a better investment than investing in our knowledge, our relationships and our future. Taking considered and calculated risks to follow our dreams is an astute investment indeed. We, more than anyone else, must believe that our personal stocks will increase in value and return substantial dividends to ourselves, our loved ones and our community, if each of us can manage, in our own unique way, to:

'Do what you believe in. Believe in what you do.'

51

'I may cry easily
but I never give up'

Greg Louganis

During every Olympic Games, many dreams are achieved or shattered in a thousandth of a second. For some, silver medals are disappointing, although being second best in the world is no shame. Others, like Britain's 'Eddie the Eagle', who competed in the ski jump event at the 1988 Calgary Winter Olympics, have their wildest dreams fulfilled, simply by competing. Eddie finished last, as did African swimmer 'Eric the Eel' at the Sydney 2000 Summer Olympics. For Eric, who had never swum in a 50-metre pool until the Olympics, winning was never an expectation—so losing was never a disappointment. These competitors enjoyed the moment more than most, as do many Paralympians, who are an example of courage to us all.

Greg Louganis has been another example of sporting and personal courage for over a quarter of a century. Not content to settle for a silver medal in diving at the 1976 Montreal Olympics, nor swayed by the US boycott of the 1980 Moscow Olympics, Louganis finally collected gold in 1984 at Los Angeles. But most will remember him for winning the 1988 diving event in Seoul after striking his head on the diving board, and plunging bloodied into the pool or, again for diving head-on into controversy when he came out of the closet a few years later and announced to the world that he was gay, and had AIDS at the time of his last Olympic victory.

Like Greg Louganis, I was adopted and, ever since I was a little girl, dreamed of being a world champion athlete. I actually aspired to be a gridiron quarterback but despite playing in an all male league, soon realised that aspiration wasn't going to happen in my lifetime! I was a slow runner, swimmer and skater so I threw myself into team sports, and represented my high school and university in basketball, volleyball and field hockey. I was a member of a national champion field hockey team, once represented Canada in international volleyball, and attended graduate school in the United States on a combined academic/basketball scholarship.

Unfortunately, I was no longer competing by the time Canada first entered teams in the Olympic women's basketball and volleyball competitions in 1976; and women's field hockey was not introduced into the Olympics until the 1980 Moscow games, so my dream of becoming an Olympic athlete, like so many other of our childhood dreams, remained only that. But the truth of the matter is that, even if I had been born a few years later, I was never a gifted athlete. I was always the kid who tried hardest and just made the team by the skin of my teeth, often contributing little more than encouragement from the bench. My parents never encouraged me in sport and we had many a domestic debate when I was forced to forgo valuable athletic practice time for what my parents saw as more lady-like pursuits, such as piano or singing lessons. When I was barred from singing in the Sunday School choir, Mum finally realised I was 'musically challenged'!

I may never have become a world-class athlete but I discovered an aptitude for sports administration, which led me into the equally competitive business world. It wasn't until the night of the closing ceremony of the 1988 Calgary Winter Olympics that I discovered where I might have inherited my passion for sport. While watching the broadcast from my hometown in Canada, on a sweltering summer's day in Sydney, Australia, I first received a letter from my biological parents and was amazed to learn that my father had been a professional athlete. In fact, he was an eight-time Canadian champion rodeo cowboy.

Shortly after that, I was present to share his pride, and that of his family, when he was inducted into the Rodeo Hall of Fame. Although I was jet lagged, the adrenaline was pumping and, long after the celebrations, I lay awake in bed wondering: 'Wow! What if I'd been raised by my biological father and been encouraged in my love of sport? Would I have fulfilled my dream of being a world champion? What if? What if?'

As I lay in the darkness of the hotel room, I fortunately came to my senses and started asking 'What if' in another way. 'Yeah, Cath...but what if you'd been born a poor child in Nepal with a life expectancy of 37? What if you'd been born without legs? What if you hadn't been born at all?'

At that moment in my life, I realised that life isn't about 'What if'. Life is about 'What is.' The 'what is' of my life was that, even though they didn't like sport, I had been blessed with the best parents in the whole world and they would always be my Mum and Dad. The 'what is' of my life was that I either wasn't good enough or wasn't dedicated enough to be a world-class athlete.

I also realised that life evolves as you grow older and it's still sometimes possible to modify childhood dreams, to re-set goals and to re-frame fantasies. So, I set my sights on attending the next Olympic Games and did so as part of the support crew for the Australian team four years later at Barcelona. A client took me to the 1996 Atlanta Olympics four years after that.

Then, at the Sydney 2000 Olympic Games, on the day of the opening ceremony, I was thrilled, honoured and humbled to carry the Olympic torch. As Sydney hosted the biggest party in its history, I couldn't help but reflect that I had never had a 21st birthday celebration because my adopted parents had died from cancer within that year. With their loss, the dreams I'd dreamed until that time were suddenly shattered. At a time when I really needed a best friend, my best friend and her husband were in Australia. So, with no immediate family, I left Canada with a backpack and $200 for a three-month working holiday in Australia, feeling vulnerable and very alone.

Little did I realise in those dark days of despair, that the biggest problem of my life would provide the biggest opportunity. I am now a dual citizen of Canada and Australia, who has been fortunate enough to play sport on every continent. I am truly grateful for all the blessings in life—even though some were heavily disguised in tough times.

What are the 'what ifs' in your life today that are holding you back from reaching your full potential?

The Olympic flame serves as a reminder to all of us to have big dreams like Pierre de Coubertin, founder of the modern Olympic Games. We must each dare to follow our dream. But, ultimately, to quote the words of a sponsor, we need to 'just do it'. We only grow as individuals if we continue to dream it, dare it and do it!

Although few of us will ever be Olympians, we all should strive for our personal best in whatever modest or magnificent endeavours we pursue. We must never settle for anything less.

I may have missed having 21st birthday celebrations that September a long time ago when I first arrived in Australia with my life at an all-time low. But, I made up for it on September 15, 2000 when my life was near an all-time high and I carried the Olympic flame on behalf of my adopted country.

As a member of the Olympic torch relay, I reveled in the pride of feeling a small part of something much bigger than myself—the international goodwill that was so readily shared in Sydney as we opened our doors and our hearts to worldwide visitors who, for a brief moment in time, shared the joys of this great Southern land.

I could barely believe that, on another September day, almost exactly one year later, terrorist tragedy struck New York and Washington. It's still hard to fully comprehend the difference in mood that we felt on the streets of Sydney, half a world away. But, reminiscent of the Olympic flame, most citizens did their best to try and rekindle the spirit of international tolerance that we had felt during the Olympic Games. We nodded at strangers and replaced road rage with united outrage at the loss of innocent lives, wherever it occurs on the globe.

Whatever our country by birth or by choice
now is the time to unite with one voice.

As we look to the future with respect for the past
and strive in the present for dreams that will last.

To reach our potential as one and a nation
Giving all a fair go without hesitation.

And regardless of religion or faith...
To keep faith... in our future, our planet and
ourselves.

It's not always easy to keep faith in ourselves in times of despair. We all remember where we were and what we were doing on September 11, 2001. I happened to be addressing more than a thousand delegates of the World Airline Entertainment Association in Brisbane, Australia. Three days later, I spoke at another conference on the outskirts of Sydney. As I stopped for petrol, another customer overheard my North American accent (still present after over twenty-five years in Australia). He tentatively touched me on the arm and stammered, 'I'm sorry'. His heavy accent was European, but his gentle gesture resonated with universal eloquence.

As I drove along, I was at a loss as to what I would say to the gathering of librarians, about customer service and managing change, because there is some change over which we simply have no control. But we do always have control over our attitude-just as I had no control over changed circumstances when my parents died, but still had control over my attitude. At that time, I could choose either to look backward and feel sorry for myself or to look forward on a new path. I didn't want sympathy, so only a handful of close friends knew that my folks had died and, unlike Greg Louganis, I never cried. (at least not in public). In hindsight, crying may have been a smarter thing to do, rather than bottling up all that emotional grief.

As most of the civilised world openly grieved as one after September 11, 2001, I realised I couldn't simply give my standard presentation on change and customer service. It became clear that we must think not just of service to our customers but to our families, our communities, our country and our planet. We must consider ourselves of service in both the tragic and the magic times.

We must ignore negativities, like the cynical signs that appeared in a few retail outlets after the Olympics:

'You can stop smiling now—they've all gone home'.

Now is the time for that unsolicited nod or smile to a stranger. Now is the time to tell friends you care and give everyone you love extra hugs—not just today but every day. Like Olympic champions, we all need to give our own personal best to challenges of conscience. Whether it be solitary meditation, or prayer, or being a little kinder to others in a crowd, let's connect our heads and hearts. We can all just do the best we can with what we've got.

Just as the Olympic flame was a symbol of hope, we must never lose a burning passion for life—doing whatever we can to live and appreciate this day the best way we can—for others and ourselves as we continue to share the spirit. No matter how tough times may seem, it's never too late to ignite *your* dream.

Sure, we may feel down in the dumps from time to time. This is a normal sign of being human and being alive. Yes, we may cry, in private or in public, and even though few of us will ever be Olympic gold medallists, we can still be champion people if we follow the maxim of Greg Louganis:

'I may cry easily but I never give up'.

52

'Create your own tomorrows with your thoughts and actions today.'

Catherine DeVrye

One of the wonderful things about being human and living in a civilised society is that we have the most incredible array of choices available every day—more than our ancestors ever dreamed possible.

It's likely that anyone reading this, no matter how they may perceive their own life at present, has a lifestyle that millions in the world would envy. It's easy to forget that some people don't even have a choice of what they read, or have never had the opportunity to learn to read.

It's also easy to take choice for granted when life isn't working out quite the way we'd planned. Sometimes we have a choice of shaping events in our lives, but unfortunately we don't always have control over those events. We would never consciously choose for ourselves or those we love to have a car accident, serious illness, job loss through a merger, or be caught in a hurricane. But, even if the worst disaster strikes, it's imperative to never forget that we still always have control over our attitudes toward those events.

When my parents both died of cancer within a year of each other, I had no choice whatsoever in the matter. However, aged 22, I was faced with a number of other choices: to feel sorry for myself or get on with my life; to seek the so-called comfort of drugs or the true support of friends; to be negative or positive; to look backward or forward.

Although I had absolutely no choice surrounding the events that preceded the sad situation I found myself in, I still had a choice in terms of what attitude I adopted. I knew that whatever choice I made wouldn't bring them back so simply chose to get on with my own life as best I could.

Admittedly, there were times when I had grave doubts that I would succeed in doing so, but there is no comparison between that which is lost by not succeeding and that which is lost by not trying. Without any family to fall back on or blame, I probably learned earlier than most that I was totally responsible for my own choices for the rest of my life. I realised that a life without dreams is like a souffle without air; a life without hope is like a rose without petals; and, a life without joy is like a symphony without sound.

I subsequently learned that choice can be limiting or liberating; entrapping or empowering; and can lead to inaction or proaction. As humans we have the gift of choosing the path we walk. Sometimes we take the wrong road, but the choice is entirely ours.

I've walked the beat with police in a rough neighbourhood as bricks were hurled at pedestrians; been called to an armed robbery; intervened in a domestic violence situation; and sat for hours on a drug bust. The perpetrators of these crimes made different choices than me, but I suspend judgment because I know I could have just as easily made the same choices and give thanks that I didn't. I also respect the police for their choice of an often-thankless career.

Choices have given me more than my fair share of joy and sorrow. But even in my darkest moments, I remind myself to give thanks for that freedom to choose.

> *Thank you for hot steamy showers*
> *And icy cold drinks*
> *Thank you for choice.*
>
> *Thank you for sunshine*
> *And snowflakes*
> *Thank you for choice.*
>
> *Thank you for speech*
> *And silence*
> *Thank you for choice.*
>
> *Thank you for superhighways*
> *And unmarked tracks*
> *Thank you for choice.*

Thank you for minds which open
And zippers that close
Thank you for choice.

Thank you for high tech
And high touch
Thank you for choice.

Thank you for water which runs
And time that stands still
Thank you for choice.

Thank you for colourful art
And black inked books
Thank you for choice.

Thank you for powerful towering pines
And gentle, clinging jasmine
Thank you for choice.

Thank you for symphonies
And surf
Thank you for choice.

Thank you for the laughter
And love—of family and friends
They give us all more choice!

Every day, I'm truly grateful for everything I have—like freedom and food. I'm equally grateful for everything I don't have—like persecution and hunger. Every day, I'm grateful for choice. Every day, it's worth reminding ourselves that we all have more choice than ever before, that we all have more choice than we think we might at the time.

Speaking of time, I know yours is valuable, so

thank you for choosing to read this book. Whatever your future choices, I wish you well on your journey and please remember that it's the choices *you* make that will help you:

'Create your own tomorrows with your thoughts and actions today.'

Acknowledgements

When we sip our hot lemon and honey, we usually overlook all the ingredients that went into that broth . . . The farmer who grew the lemons and the apiarist who tended the bees, the distributor who brought the lemons to market, the production line that manufactured the honey jars, the quality control staff who processed the honey for our hygiene, the staff in the supermarket where we bought the end product. The list goes on and we may only be familiar with a brand name. So too with publishing, we may only know the author but many unsung heroes bring a book to market.

I sincerely thank Josh Dowse, Patrick Gallacher and the entire team at Allen & Unwin for their excellence in the initial development and publication of this book; DiZign and Scharlaine Cairns for design and editing of the revised edition;

235

Mediaworks International for the promotion; and the media for their great coverage. Also, to my own team for invaluable behind the scenes support, especially Fiona Stuart, Liz Lynn and Jan Hallett.

Grateful appreciation to literary agent Shelia Drummond; export consultant Richard Yabsley; and Austrade for their help to have this Australian book subsequently translated to global markets. And, to the moral support of other writers like Ellie Brown, Roy Carlisle, Kris Cole, Bryce Courtenay, Margaret Gee, Julie Harris, Bret Witter and the team at the Maui Writers retreat.

You can lead someone to hot lemon and honey but you can't make them drink. So, thank you in advance to anyone who's bought the book. Without readers, there would be little reason to be an author! Thanks also to the thousands of staff in bookstores, both physical and on line, who bring the reader such a wide choice of produce to market.

I'd like to acknowledge everyone who's ever been my employer or employee; client or colleague; supplier or supporter. There are too many to name in over three decades of working life. Some are still close friends, some I've sadly lost contact with and some I hope to never see again! Still, I'm pleased we've all shared the journey to date, even if the only thing I learned from some was that I never wanted to follow their path.

Over the years, employers like Pat Tritter, Wally Schwank, Doug Neville, Bert Keddie, Brian Dixon,

Alex McCartney, Ver Pena and Roy Lea have provided soothing sips of inspiration and wisdom for me. From my first boss to my last, these folks have simultaneously been my managers, mentors and 'mates'.

My appreciation also goes to the many clients and bureaus who have booked me to speak over the years. I value your business and, in many cases, your ongoing friendship; a special note of appreciation to Debbie Tawse of Celebrity Speakers New Zealand for her help on this project. Thanks to other people who I may have never met but who heard me speak and have sent unsolicited letters or emails, sharing their thoughts and juicy tidbits of information, commenting on what's been relevant to them from my other books or presentations.

Similarly, I've been inspired by the writings and achievements of Jack Canfield and Sir Edmund Hillary, and thank them for taking time out of their busy schedules to comment on this book.

A lifetime of gratitude goes to *all* my friends who tolerate my absences from social functions because of deadlines or travel commitments; especially to Alan, Frank, Liz, Kay, Kristine, Kim and June who constantly remind me about maintaining the balance in my own life. Like Dad, with his silent support and Mum, with her hot lemon and honey, they're the ones always there to help me keep a clear head.

Catherine DeVrye

We sincerely hope that you've found the words in this book both timely and timeless.

You can contribute to the next book, *A Second Sip of Hot Lemon and Honey,* by expanding on your favourite quote in 500 words or less. If used, you'll not only receive an acknowledgment but a free copy of the book. Contact www.greatmotivation.com

For further information on Catherine DeVrye's other books and her availability to customise a presentation for your next conference, please contact:

www.greatmotivation.com
Everest Press
PO Box 559
Manly NSW 1655 Australia
Phone 61-2-9977 3177
Fax 61-2-9977 3122
Email books@greatmotivation.com

Other books, audio and postcards by Catherine DeVrye

Discounts available for bulk orders.

Let us know if you'd like a signed copy for someone special.

- *Hot Lemon & Honey* – audio presentation.
- *Hope Happens! ... words of encouragement for tough times.* A best-selling inspirational gift book.
- *Hope as my Compass/Who Says I Can't?...a memoir.* (in North America as Serendipity Road). Bryce Courtenay says: 'story of hope and perseverance – when's the movie?'.
- *Nature of Resilience- words for life in times of strife.*
- *Good Service is Good Business: 7 Simple Strategies for Success.* One of Australia's best-selling business books, filled with practical examples.
- *Good Service is Good Business: Audio CDs from* the author's popular radio drive-time series, plus staff training kit.
- *The Customer Service Zoo: Create Customers for Life and a Life for Yourself.* A parable using animal analogies to simplify and inspire your customer service.
- *Japan: An A-Z Guide of Living and Working in Japan.* Practical suggestions for those travelling to Japan or working with the Japanese.
- *Paperclips Don't Grow on Tress* - add value, not cost to your bottom line.
- *Motivational postcards* with colourful photographs and powerful quotes.

Not everyone in the world has been as fortunate as me so I hope that some royalties from this book may make a modest contribution to the mammoth mission of the Himalayan Trust—a non-profit organisation founded by the late Sir Edmund Hillary to build hospitals and schools in Nepal. His continuous contribution since he first set foot on Everest in 1953 leaves a legacy and a lesson to us all. Donations can be made to:

The Australian Himalayan Foundation.
www.australianhimalayanfoundation.org.au

240

'Let others praise ancient times.
I am glad I was born in these.'

Ovid 43BC–AD18